HOLY WARRIORS

I strongly recommend this timely book as a comprehensive, scholarly and sensitive analysis of Islam and the militant ideology of Islamism.

Since September 11, those of us who live in the 'West' have realised that we must develop an appropriate response which will enable us to live peacefully and in friendship with our Muslim neighbours in our own countries and throughout the world, while developing an appropriate response to the very real threats posed by militant theology and Islamist terrorism.

This book will help to inform our thinking in developing a sensitive and spiritual, political and personal response to the complex issues which confront us.'

Baroness Cox, House of Lords.

HOLY WARRIORS

Frog and Amy Orr-Ewing

Authentic
LIFESTYLE

First published 2002 by Authentic Lifestyle

7 6 5 4 3 2 1   08 07 06 05 04 03 02

Authentic Lifestyle is an imprint of Authentic Media
PO Box 300, Carlisle, Cumbria CA3 0QS
and PO Box 1047, Waynesboro, GA 30830-2047
www.paternoster-publishing.com

British Library Cataloguing in Publication Data

A catalogue record for this book is available from the British
Library

1-85078-460-4

Cover design by Gerald Rogers
Printed in Great Britain by Cox and Wyman, Reading

Contents

Dedication

This book is dedicated to Miles and Sarah, "Your love has given us great joy and encouragement because you have refreshed the hearts of the saints."

And to Hartmut and Jane - the faith that first lived in you now lives in us.

Acknowledgements

There are so many people who have inspired and helped us over the last few years. Space is limited here but we would love to specifically thank a few people. Thanks to James Nichols for kind help in times of need, Antje for your prayers for us, Colin Orr-Ewing for having all those incredible telephone numbers to hand, Geoff B. the friendly face of Ashkabad, Al and Gareth Cook for proof reading and lots of laughs, and Tim Bradshaw for encouragement and opportunities. Thank you to David Zeiden, Lucy Atherton, Kate Young, Robin Parry, and all those at Authentic for help with the manuscript. Thank you to Dee and Bridget we love you very much. Thank you to the congregation of St Aldate's Church for your nurture while we were students, and your love over the last few years. Thank you to The Barnabas Fund, Christian Solidarity Worldwide and Open Doors for your inspiring and tireless work on behalf of the persecuted church. Thank you to Michael, Anne, Joe, Elaine, Moyne, Tim, John and Heather for your love and support. The Zacharias Trust is truly blessed with such a family. Special thanks to Ravi and Margie Zacharias – we count it a privilege to work with you. Thank you also to the wider RZIM family in the USA, India, Singapore and Canada. Thank you to the many friends who have cared for us, including Andy and Sylvia Lawson Johnston for untiring love; Yong Yeow for lasting friendship; Barney de Berry for rock solid encouragement and Olivia and James Shone prayer partners from first to last. We would finally like to give thanks and devotion to our wonderful Saviour.

Foreword

For several years now, it has been my privilege to know Frog and Amy. It is rare to meet people who have both a love for ideas and a love for people, and this book demonstrates their love for both. Increasingly, people are asking more and more searching questions about Islam, and this requires a carefully researched critique of what Islam has to say. This is what this book does. However, this manuscript is no ivory tower exercise. Frog and Amy have travelled extensively, talked to people we could not even imagine meeting, and prayed earnestly for people and with people from Islamic countries. The book is worth reading if only for their own personal recollections of their travels.

By looking at the historical origins, growth and development of Islam, Frog and Amy introduce you the original sources, early commentary and interpretation, and later development of the teachings of the Qur'an. Having studied Islam whilst at Oxford, they bring contemporary scholarship to bear on the current discussion about Islam and make it accessible to the ordinary reader.

What is of particular interest is their understanding of Afghanistan and the Taliban, a subject on which everyone today has an opinion. Their insight however has not been pieced together through the collection of newspaper cuttings and television news clips. They have been there, met with some of the leadership, shared their own convictions about Christ, and lived to tell the tale. You will enjoy this book as I have.

Michael Ramsden

Introduction

Islam is a hot topic in Western society today. This is a religion that provokes strong reactions both in its critical observers and its committed adherents. Islam is not monolithic; in fact there are many diverse expressions of it around the world. In this book we want to examine the emergent radical expression of Islam which has burst into Western consciousness. We attempt to bring a fresh perspective by asking theological and ideological questions of extreme Islam rather than focusing solely on socioeconomic motivations. Our understanding of radical Islam is drawn from personal experience of various expressions of Islam.

This book intends to provide a fresh perspective on militant Islam in the world today. We aim to help readers understand this new phenomenon in its theological context within Islam and also in its relation to the West. We ask the question: Do the ideas of extremist Muslims find precedent or justification in the scriptures or history of Islam?

A particular window was opened for us on these matters through visiting the Taliban leaders in Herat, Afghanistan, in 1996. Our lives became intertwined with the Taliban long before the twin towers were destroyed and the appalling attacks on America wreaked their havoc. For much of the Western press, the Taliban have always been just another radical Islamic regime, renowned for their mistreatment of women and their ultra-orthodoxy. Now, however, images of the Taliban are deeply ingrained in the visual imagination of the Western world. Some see the women in grey burkas – the full-body veil with a grill to see through – when they think of the Taliban. For others, the early images of televisions and videotapes strewn across the streets of Kabul represent their deep antipathy to Western values.

Our own contact with Islam begins with Amy's experience of growing up as a Christian in a multicultural British context. Her family lived in a vicarage in Sparkhill, in inner-city Birmingham. This is just one of many city-centre areas of this country where the Islamic community is a significant minority. The reality of forced arranged marriages and traditional expectations of women stand out in Amy's memory. Through dialogue and friendship with local Muslim friends she gained first-hand experience of the beliefs and practices of Islam.

During her school holidays Amy also toured many different countries where Islam was the predominant world-view – including Morocco, Uzbekistan and Kazakhstan – with a Christian performing arts group. Through these experiences, she felt a growing sense of compassion and understanding for those of the Muslim faith. She began to pray regularly for the people of Afghanistan in particular, that the Mujahedin would hear the wonderful good news of how it is possible to have a relationship with God through Christ.

Both of us studied theology at Oxford University, went to the same church and belonged to the Christian Union there. We eventually met at a weekly 7.30 a.m. prayer group that Amy had started in order to pray for churches in Central Asia and China. The following summer we travelled through China as part of a group of eight undergraduates, spending most of our time in Xinjiang (China's northwestern province). Xinjiang includes parts of the Gobi Desert and is home to the largely unknown Central Asian ethnic communities of China, including several million Uygurs.

The Uygurs have tried unsuccessfully to hold out against Chinese control of their region. Although there has been a Christian witness among them for several centuries, the majority has followed Islam since the eighth century. Their expression of Islam is highly unorthodox, partly because of the enduring Chinese communist policy of suppressing religion. Most of the Uygur mosques and theological schools have been closed or have leaders sympathetic to communist policy. In a town called Yining (only a few miles from the border with

Kazakhstan), for example, the focus of religious devotion is not the mosque but the cemetery, which spreads across the hill overlooking the town. This is the locus of spirituality for many of the Islamic Uygurs, and they go there regularly to pray and visit the graves of their relations and ancestors. The culture of the Uygurs is wonderfully rich, and they are famous for bright fabrics and fantastically tasty kebabs and Nan bread.

Also in this province, which shares a narrow section of border with Afghanistan, are many Uzbeks, Kazakhs and Tajiks, all of whom now have their own nations in the neighbouring ex-Soviet states. Uygur nationalism is on the rise. The people are drawing out their suppressed Islamic identity, and the example of neighbouring communities is encouraging them in their struggle. Add to this a justifiable grievance at their subjection to a Chinese apartheid, and the fact that their region has been plundered of vast resources in rich oil and mineral supplies, and one can see how social and political factors could affect a politically extreme form of Islam. The evidence of this extremism at present can be seen in a number of bombings in Urumqi, the province's capital.

While in China in 1995, three of us began to plan a trip to Afghanistan. When we returned to England we discovered that only a few months earlier many of the aid agencies had temporarily moved out of Afghanistan – some for their own safety, and others in indignation. The UNICEF project, for example, was headed up by a woman. She was not allowed to meet with the Taliban because of her gender, and this made much of UNICEF's continued work in the region unfeasible. These stringent policies against women brought the Taliban into the Western limelight in the mid-1990s.

We read as much literature as we could in preparation for our trip to Afghanistan in Easter 1996, needless to say, not without a certain trepidation and nervousness. The borders were closed, the Foreign Office did not recommend visiting the country now that it was controlled by the Taliban and in the midst of a civil war. The only way to get a visa into the country was as an aid worker or a journalist. The next difficulty was getting there from England. Iran wasn't particularly accessible, and their border was closed. Pakistan was possible, but we wanted to visit northwestern Afghanistan. The only option for entry seemed to be one of the ex-Soviet states bordering Afghanistan.

Not many people made the journey from Britain into Turkmenistan in early 1996. Only a handful of expatriates, mostly involved in the oil business, lived in the country. The rough terrain and hostile environment made it an unattractive location to stay in for long. Theoretically, one could only enter the country on business, and our business credentials, as theology undergraduates, were even shakier than our journalism credentials! Our friend Miles was the odd one out, as he had finished at Oxford University and was employed in marketing. The end result was that, though we could fly to Ashkabad, the capital of Turkmenistan, we couldn't get a visa for that country or for Afghanistan.

We gave some thought to the thorny question of how to get the visa into Afghanistan. How does one become a journalist or an aid worker at short notice? A friend of Frog's called Rob had become programme controller for "Oxygen", the Oxford student radio station (which has since folded – nothing to do with us), and he found himself in dire need of foreign correspondents in Afghanistan. The student newspaper "The Cherwell" also found that they had this need, and very soon we had two letters declaring our credentials, which we presented to the Afghan embassy in London. The slightly astonished lady chall-enged us, asking if we were aware of the civil war going on in the country. She was adamant that she couldn't allow a woman into Afghanistan. We were insistent, but the consulate must have hoped we would forget about the whole idea, for they delayed and delayed.

The day before our flights arrived, and we still had no visa for Afghanistan or Turkmenistan. Geoff, a contact at the British Consulate in Turkmenistan, told us there was a fifty-fifty chance of getting a visa at the airport – but that you could never tell which fifty you might get. He advised us to stay put. That afternoon, after badgering the Afghan Embassy, the lady we had been dealing with explained all the risks again and finally said they might give us a visa on the condition that we signed a letter saying that we were going against their advice. We dutifully wrote and signed the letter – our lives were in God's hands, and we couldn't rely on the Afghan government or its representatives to rescue us if there was any trouble. They reluctantly gave us our visas on the morning of our flight.

Our flight to Ashkabad was fairly uneventful, although Miles did sit next to an Indiana Jones-type archaeologist from Sheffield whose specialty was finding lost cities in the desert. He gave us the reassuring news that hotels cost about $250 per night. So we had a visa but only enough money to last three nights!

As we had prayed and hoped, the visa regime was more "flexible", and we were allowed a few days in the country. When we arrived at the airport we were surprised and happy to be met by somebody asking, "Are you Mr Orr-Ewing?" Geoff, despite warning us not to come, had in fact turned up to meet us and to help us find a hotel.

We all still remember the taxi ride around town – one hotel after the other seemed "a little beyond our budget". The final possibility was only $50 a night. The hotel was dirty and attended by a tea lady on each floor who eavesdropped and checked up on everyone – a skill learned in Soviet training, no doubt.

On every public building in Turkmenistan, the self-styled leader of the Turkmen, called "Turkmenbasy", was emblazoned in grim splendour. Some of the vestiges of communism remained, and we were watched carefully wherever we went. But on the first day in our hotel there was a telephone call for us. A lady on the other end said: "I believe you have just arrived in Ashkabad, welcome. Would you be interested in renting an apartment for the few days you are here, with two bedrooms?" and she quoted a price significantly lower than our hotel bill. When we expressed our interest, she said: "Meet me at the circus at four o'clock. My name is Angela and I will be wearing a green dress." With that, she put the phone down.

We met Angela and found the apartment clean and safe. After settling into our rooms, we began to plan for our journey to the Afghan border. With the help of a phrase book and a wonderful taxi driver we managed to purchase tickets for the train to the Turkmen-Afghan border town of Kushka. The train journey – 18 hours of slow motion through desert and small towns with a lamb crying in a lady's hand luggage all the way – was an experience in itself. When we eventually arrived at the Kushka station we had to walk for about two miles to find the border. As we asked directions, people laughed at us and warned us about the war.

When we finally reached the border, we found a metal walkway stretched over the road with a solitary ex-Soviet soldier walking backwards and forwards like an extra from a grainy war film – except that this soldier was armed only with a knife. We can only guess that the soldier had exceptional aim and so would be able to prevent someone from crossing that border without authorization. A group was lounging on a bank beside the border post waiting for something – to cross, or for others to join them, or for the price of bribes to come down. Three backpacking Westerners entering the war zone was obviously their idea of a joke: for they fell about laughing and playing with imaginary machine guns and faking explosions as we approached and waited beside them.

The borders into Central Asia are popular for drug trafficking – approximately 80 per cent of Europe's heroin has come from Afghanistan through this route. Large trucks laden with goods were waved through – some received a cursory check, though we suspected that this was for the sole benefit of our Western eyes, because the truck drivers seemed very surprised.

After an "appropriate" wait of over an hour, the three of us were ushered into the border cabin and our backpacks were put through an enormous hand-cranked X-ray machine, and we were interrogated for nearly two hours. The longer we waited the more nervous we became, because we had heard there was a curfew in Afghanistan. We didn't really want night to fall before we were safely in a hotel somewhere in Afghanistan. Where could we stay in the town? The reply: "If there is a hotel still standing, you can stay there." Great.

On the other side of this border hut we found not Afghanistan, but a bridge and half a mile of road through no man's land. We put our bags onto a large flat trolley (perhaps normally used for ferrying drugs?) and strolled into this no man's land. (We had been laughed at when we asked about the bus mentioned in our guidebook "that goes regularly from the border to the nearest town".) The road was pock-marked, and flame-licked ruins could be seen in the distance. The detritus of war lay around. But all was quiet.

As we walked on the officious Soviet atmosphere began to ebb, and terror gave way to a feeling of adventure. We saw a chain stretched across the road, and an old container with a door in it – the Afghan border post. A ramshackle bunch of Afghan soldiers smiled broadly – they were handsome, and some had piercing, clear blue eyes. One opened his arms wide and said, "Welcome to Afghanistan". Frog became the spokesman and was ushered into the shed while a chair was brought out into the open desert for Miles, and 30 men gathered around him in a wide circle, watching. There was no chair for Amy, now swathed in a headscarf and living in an exclusion zone. She felt that they were scared to come near her. In the shed, Frog got the visas stamped and haggled for a ride to the city.

During this journey to the city it became clear that the bulk of those at the border were not actually Taliban. Our driver put Hindi pop music into his stereo, and made fond references to Kabul discos and Johnny Walker. Whenever we came to the frequent roadblocks, he would put on a peaked hat, switch off the stereo and look sombre and official. He was actually a civil servant and got us through each checkpoint with no hassle. Once past each roadblock, he would take off the hat, put the stereo back on and proclaim: 'Taliban – Donkeys. Ha!' We drove most of the way at a crawl because of the craters in the road. One bridge we drove over had such massive holes in it that we could see the river underneath us. The Soviets had blown up much of the infrastructure as they left. We saw wrecks of tanks and a helicopter rotor-blade on one side of the road, while on the other side the grass was long – the minefields.

He brought us to the city with half an hour to spare before the curfew, and we found a small hostel, which for a night we shared with a Chinese American journalist. He was grumpy because John Simpson of the BBC was in town and no other journalists could get a look in.

As journalists we wanted to get an interview with the Taliban leaders, and so we went to a café that the Taliban were known to frequent. As we walked in together countless eyes turned, shocked that Amy was coming with us – a blonde woman in male territory. Many Taliban personnel were in the room, basking like colonials over their newly conquered city. They looked poor and dirty, though some were clothed in white, and all had the distinctive scarves slung over their shoulders. We played language games and arranged, some-how, to have a translator for an interview with the Taliban leaders the next day.

When the next day came, we realized that our request hadn't really been understood. The language games went on for an hour and a crowd of nearly 60 Taliban gathered around our table – though they never came within five feet of Amy, who was still in her exclusion zone. The conversation became heated as they tried to convert us to Islam. The *kalashnikovs* casually slung over their shoulders began to take on a new significance. They offered us Coca-Cola that we politely refused. With further persuasion we found ourselves drinking the cola – it had no label, was made locally, and tasted like ani-mal fat. A simple vocabulary mistake of host-hostage rather than host-guest disturbed us for a few moments.

Just when the situation was beginning to feel extremely tense, the Pakistani translator arrived. He had arranged a vehicle to take us to meet the Taliban leaders. We were bun-dled in and driven off out of the city. We were taken to the headquarters building, where the education minister of the region met us. He was sweating profusely and shaking and appeared to be detoxing. Through reading and research we later discovered that the Taliban gained a large proportion of their income through the international drugs trade. These Taliban leaders were initially dubious about allowing Amy into the building, but surprisingly, relented when Frog and Miles explained that they feared for her safety.

We were ushered into a dark room with bedrolls and mattresses strewn around the floor. Frog and Miles sat with the group assembled. One of the men was the Foreign Minister, another was the Keeper of the Holy Qur'an, and another two men were assistants of some kind. Each one was humbly dressed with the characteristic draped scarves on their heads. Amy sat silently, separate from the rest of the group, with her head and face covered and the interview began.

We asked many questions; were they religious students? Where had they studied? None were from Herat the town that we were visiting. What languages did they speak? Pushtu, Urdu and Arabic – although none could speak the local language Farsi. What schools of theology were they influenced by? The reply was, "None – the Qur'an alone is our guiding light." What were their intentions? "To establish pure Islam and Shariah law in the whole of Afghanistan." These Taliban leaders expressed no military ambitions beyond the borders of Afghanistan. What message did they have for Muslims living in the West? "They should come to Afghanistan and help." What message did they have for Western leaders? "Tell your Queen that she must become a Muslim."

The Taliban were warm and generous to us in their hospitality; after about an hour they brought some food which they dubbed 'Herat burgers'. During the course of the interview the Taliban broke for their prayers, which they completed in front of us. Bowing down towards Mecca, the fervency and suddenness of their prayer startled us. After this our interview resumed and we explained that we too were students of religion and that we had studied Islam. They were very keen for us to spend a night as their guests and after many apologies we were able to make our way back to our hotel. Before leaving we gave each religious leader a copy of the Bible which they accepted graciously and enthusiastically.

During the course of the trip we met a number of local townspeople and interviewed them about Islam and the Taliban: some of their comments and observations find their way into this book. Many were frightened of the Taliban and did not feel able to give their names. Complaints reached us about such diverse grievances as the termination of education and employment for women, having to pray too often and giving up alcohol, beards and music. We also encountered wealthy Saudi Arabian businessmen, driving Mercedes with tinted windows through the dusty streets of Herat – the evidence of significant foreign support for Taliban rule was ominous and undeniable.

For us the Taliban represented a genuine religious zeal whose quest for pure Islam, expressed both in the heart of the individual and in society, resulted in a political and religious system which was menacing and oppressive.

1

An Introduction to Islam

This chapter will give a broad introduction to the theology, history and practices of Islam. The intention is that the reader may gain an overview within which the more radical expressions of the faith find their place. This survey will introduce many of the themes that will be referred to in following chapters, and should provide a foundation for later discussion.

Muhammad

The founder of the Islamic faith, Muhammad, was born around AD 570. Collections of anecdotes of the life of Muhammad which were compiled after his death called "Hadith" tell us that his father died before he was born and his mother died when he was still a young child. When his grandfather also died he was taken care of by his Uncle Abu Talib. Muhammad was born into the Hashim family who were part of the powerful Quraysh tribe in Mecca. However his Uncle was not particularly prosperous and Muhammad worked as a child helping as a shepherd and a trader.

As an adult Muhammad worked as a commercial agent for a rich widow, Khadijah, who put him in charge of her caravans. He did well and although she was much older than Muhammad, she went on to marry him when he was 25. Little information about this stage of Muhammad's life is known, apart from the fact that their marriage was happy. Khadijah

bore Muhammad two sons who died in infancy and four sur-
viving daughters.

Mecca was a predominantly pagan city where various idols
and deities were worshipped. In keeping with the practice of
local pagan customs, Muhammad was in the habit of going
away to a secluded place on Mount Hira to think and pray for
one month of each year. On one such occasion he had a dream
that the angel Gabriel appeared to him and taught him some
words which now appear in the 96th Sura of the Qur'an. He
began to have visions like this around the age of 40 and he initially found them terrifying. Muhammad was convinced that
he was being possessed by an evil spirit. It was his wife
Khadijah who encouraged him to see these experiences as revelation. He stayed in Mecca for about 15 years receiving more
messages which he began to preach. His message was in general terms a call to believe in one God, to practice charity to the
poor and a warning about the final judgement of God. In the
polytheistic context of Mecca the response to his preaching
outside of his own family was small. Muhammad began to
look for patronage and protection for the small following of
the new religion and in AD 622 he took about 200 followers to
the richer Arabian city of Medina.

In Medina, Muhammad and his message proved to be more
popular than had previously been the case. From a religious
point of view Medinans were more inclined to monotheism
due to the influence of Jewish tribes in the area. Over the
course of the next years in Medina, Muhammad emerged as a
forceful religious and political leader. He unified the various
factions with a treaty called the Constitution of Medina under
which the various tribes of the area agreed to co-exist peacefully and to support each other in the event of an attack from
outside. This legal document established Muhammad as a
prophet who had civil authority to settle disputes and act as a
judge.

In Medina, Muhammad explicitly targeted Jews with his
preaching and was initially very positive about the Jews –
clearly stating that "People of the Book" would be saved (Sura
2:59). But they found his inaccurate remarks about the Old

Testament off-putting (for example, Haman is a minister of Pharaoh in Sura 40:39 and Ezra as the son of God in Sura 9:30) and very few became Muslims. As a result, he became aggressive towards the Jews, and "he was driven to allege that the Jews had corrupted, or at least misquoted, their own scriptures."[1] In Sura 2:70–3 Muhammad admonishes the Jews: "There is a party of them that heard God's word and then tampered with it ... Woe to those who write the Book with their hands, then say 'This is from God'." Muhammad also changed the direction of prayer from Jerusalem to Mecca and replaced the Jewish fast of Ashura with a fast over the whole month of Ramadan.

Having unified the tribes of Medina, Muhammad sanctioned the raiding of Meccan caravans and in fact led many of these raids personally. One of these raids proved particularly significant. In 624 at a place called Badr, Muhammad accompanied by 300 fighters attacked a large Meccan caravan. However the Meccans had anticipated this and had marshalled 950 troops to put an end to the problem. Despite being outnumbered, the Muslim army triumphed, with superior military skills and Muhammad took this victory as a divine vindication of his prophethood and leadership. The jubilation and confidence inspired by this event is reflected in Sura 8:65 "O Prophet, urge on the believers to the fight. If there are twenty among you... they will vanquish two hundred: if a hundred, they will vanquish a thousand unbelievers."

Greatly strengthened by this victory at Badr, Muhammad eliminated his opponents in Medina assassinating the poets who had satirized him and expelling one of the three Jewish tribes there.[2] This period was followed by further battles with the Meccans who now realized the full threat that Muhammad potentially posed. Muhammad suffered a number of setbacks including the loss of a battle at Uhud and the besieging of Medina by a confederacy of ten thousand men in 627. However, due to a combination of secret negotiations with various factions, the confederacy began to break up and compounded by appalling weather conditions the besiegers withdrew.

By 630 Medina had grown in wealth and power within Arabia and under the leadership of Muhammad the Medinans captured Mecca. From this position Muhammad was able to consolidate his power and concentrate on the conversion of the Bedouin and most of Arabia to Islam.

Islamic Perspectives on Muhammad

Muhammad's place in Islamic thinking is one of high honour. He is presented in the Qur'an as a mere human being but the most elevated human that will ever live. Prophethood itself is seen as the height of Allah's activity in the world and so to be the last and greatest of all prophets was the most significant honour which could be given by God to a human. The *Hadith* are written collections of the oral traditions of the sayings and action of Muhammad. One *Hadith* demonstrates Muhammad's view of himself:

> I have been granted excellence over the other prophets in six things: the earth has been made a mosque for me, with its soil declared pure; booty has been made lawful for me; I have been given victory through the inspiring awe at the distance of a month's journey; I have been given permission to intercede; I have been sent to all mankind; and the prophets have been sealed with me.[3]

Although Muhammad is not considered divine in orthodox Islam, the honour given to him by many Muslims goes beyond the bounds of the Qur'an. One important example of this is the popular tradition that Muhammad will act as an intercessor on judgement day. There are thousands of Islamic poems and prayers which express the hope that Muhammad's intercession will win them salvation. Muhammad's place in Islamic spirituality in modern-day Pakistan illustrates the tendency to venerate him:

> Muhammad veneration is projected through the mass media, schoolbooks and cultural events all of which contribute to the

deification of the Arabian Prophet. The following examples illustrate this point: 'Though my link with the Divinity of God be severed, May my hand never let go of the hem of the Chosen One.'⁴

However much Muhammad is eulogized and deified in popular Islam the fact remains that the central and overarching teaching of Islam is that God is one person.

The God of Islam: Allah

The question "Who is God?" can be answered in a number of ways within Islam and flowing from various passages of the Qur'an we find "the ninety-nine beautiful names"⁵ for Allah. Sura 59:22–4 expresses it in this way:

> He is God; there is no god but He. He is the knower of the Unseen and the Visible; He is the All-merciful, the All-compassionate. He is God; there is no other god but He. He is the King, the All-Holy, the All-peaceable, the All-faithful, the All-preserver, the All-mighty, the All-compeller, the All-sublime. Glory be to God!

There are many other passages within the Qur'an which list the names of God, and all try to express something of the majesty and beauty of God, emphasizing the awe with which he is worshipped by Muslims. The names are a key devotional element of global Islam.

However, the doctrine of God within Islam is most significantly encapsulated in the important term *Tauhid*. This word refers to faith in the principle which is at the very heart of Islam – the concept of Allah as one. God is unity itself. A universal Islamic declaration was made at the opening of the International Islamic Conference on 12 April 1980, affirming that:

> Oneness of Allah (*Tauhid*) is the foundation of Islam. It affirms that Allah and Allah alone is our Creator, Sustainer, Guide and Lord: that He has no partners: that His will is supreme and encompasses

the entire universe; that He is the Law Giver and to Him we must submit and surrender.

This concept of *Tauhid* implies that there are no distinctions based on race, colour, caste, lineage, wealth or power, since all human beings are equal in the sight of Allah. The oneness of Allah must also lead to a unity of life for the Muslim – all distinctions between the spiritual and the physical, the religious and the secular, are eliminated. For, under *Tauhid*, the whole fabric of life is governed by one goal – the realization of the divine will. Muslims believe that ever since the beginning of creation Allah sent his prophets, who conveyed his will to the rest of humankind.

The Five Pillars of Islam

The general tone of the Qur'an is sombre and meditative, because its purpose is to be a dialogue between Allah and humanity. At its core lies moral earnestness – the human response to Allah must be a life of *al-adl* (equilibrium) and *al-ahsan* (compassion). A life based on these ideas should be a balanced one. The five 'pillars' of Islam sum up the essence of *Tauhid*, or faith in one God and in his unity. They are:

1) Recitation of the confession of faith (Shahadat)
2) Observance of prayers (Salat)
3) Giving alms to the poor (Zakat)
4) An obligatory fast for adults and the physically fit in the month of Ramadan (Saum)
5) A pilgrimage to Mecca at least once in a lifetime (Hajj)

Salat, or the daily prayers, serve as a constant reminder of the transitory nature of life and of *Tauhid*. Saum, or fasting during the month of Ramadan to develop moral and physical discipline, again serves as a reminder of *Tauhid*. Zakat, or the redistribution of wealth to the poorer sections of society, reminds the Muslim of the equality of all human beings before the One God and faith in him, which is *Tauhid*. The Hajj, or pilgrimage, represents among other things the Muslim *Umma*, or the community of faith and a symbol of unity to the world. The Hajj seems to be the ultimate working out of the *Tauhid* in the corporate life of the Muslim com-munity. Faith in the one-ness of God is, therefore, a crucial concept in Islam, and one which forms the basis for practice and thinking both at the level of the individual and of the community.

Idolatry

The converse of this principle of *Tauhid* is the forbidden notion of *shirk*. *Shirk* means the association of other beings with God and in Islam it is the greatest sin – this is because it violates the central doctrine of *Tauhid*, the belief in God's unity. *Shirk* refers to the association of other beings with God. Although *shirk* may be translated as 'idolatry', this appears adequate only when exploring the early meaning of the term in Islam. At first, *shirk* was primarily understood as assoc-iating Allah's name with other deities as Muslims attacked belief in the tribal gods of pre-Islamic Arabia. After Muhammad had con-tact with Christians, the doctrine of the Trinity also came under attack and was referred to as *shirk*. The step from denouncing any association of lesser deities with Allah to the censure of any exaltation of humanity was not difficult. The Qur'an denounces any glorification of Jesus: "They are unbe-lievers who said, 'God is the Messiah, Mary's son'" (5:76).

Shirk, or putting anything in the same place as God, is a very serious matter for Muslims and a sin that must be avoid-ed at all costs. The unity of God and the strong commitment to avoid associating any other gods with him is at the very heart of the Islamic faith.

Allah as the Author of Good and Evil

Within Islam absolute monotheism is upheld. Allah is one and there is no other god or anything in creation that can be assigned as part of him or equal with him. One of the most serious sins within Islam is that of *shirk*. Allah is given many beautiful names within the Qur'an which reflect his character and actions – and he is an absolute transcendent being who is the author of both good and evil.

Among the statements in the Qur'an about God this might surprise the non-Muslim. Allah is portrayed as the author of both good and evil because he predetermines everything – both good and evil: "Whomsoever God guides, he is rightly guided; and whom he leads astray they are the losers. We have created for Gehenna many jinn and men" (7:178). The issues surrounding the moral character of Allah are discussed in the Hadith by Muhammad and his companions. It was reported that a crowd were disputing and when Muhammad asked them what the difficulty was they explained:

> Abu Bakr asserts that Allah decrees good but does not decree evil, but Umar says that He decrees both alike.' Muhammad replied to this: 'The decree necessarily determines all that is good and all that is sweet and all that is bitter, and that is my decision between you … O Abu Bakr if Allah Most High had not willed that there be disobedience, He would not have created the Devil.[6]

Revelation in the Qur'an

The Islamic view of divine revelation is that in successive generations Allah revealed himself through prophets. These human beings were men of good character who were chosen to convey a divine message in particular contexts. The Muslim conviction is that each of these prophets although raised up at different times and in different communities, such as Moses or Jesus, all had the same basic message. This message was to call people to believe in the oneness of God, to submit to his Law and do good works with the Judgement of God in mind.

The Qur'an is believed to be the final revelation of Allah to human beings and it comes through the final prophet of Islam

– Muhammad. In the text of the Qur'an the prophets who came before are alluded to, indeed many biblical names are mentioned as are various Arabian reformers from neighbouring vicinities. However, the supremacy of the revelation of the Qur'an is consistently emphasized as is the supremacy of the prophet who received the revelations.

The Text of the Qur'an

Muhammad did not write down his revelations but preached them and passed them on orally. Because of this, after Muhammad's death, it became increasingly important that the scattered pieces of revelation be gathered into a coherent whole, which could be used by the growing Muslim community. The process of compiling the Qur'an is recorded by Islamic tradition. According to this tradition, Muhammad received the different passages of the Qur'an verbatim from the angel Gabriel over a period of twenty-three years (25:35, 17:106). Having received the words, Muhammad would then recite them to the community who in turn memorized them. Scribes would copy down the words on to scraps of paper, stones, palm leaves or bits of leather. These pieces of writing were then collected together by Zayd ibn Thabit, one of Muhammad's trusted scribes. This is described in the *Hadith*:

> Then Abu Bakr said, 'You are a wise young man and we do not have any suspicion about you, and you used to write the Divine Inspiration for Allah's Apostle. So you should search for the Qur'an and collect it.'... So I started looking for the Qur'an and collecting it from palm-leaf stalks, thin white stones and also from the men who knew it by heart.[7]

However during the reign of 'Uthman, the third Muslim Caliph, it came to his attention that different Islamic communities were using slightly different versions of the Qur'an. Zayd was again chosen to oversee the project of confirming the authoritative version of the Qur'an. Again, the *Hadith* records tell us what happened:

'Uthman sent a message to Hafsa saying, 'Send us the manuscripts of the Qur'an so that we may compile the Qur'anic
materials in perfect copies and return the manuscripts to you.'
Hafsa sent it to 'Uthman. 'Uthman then ordered Zaid bin
Thabit, 'Abdullah bin Az-Zubair, Sa'id bin Al-As, and 'Abdur-
Rahman bin Harith bin Hisham to rewrite the manuscripts in
perfect copies ... When they had written many copies,
'Uthman returned the original manuscript to Hafsa. 'Uthman
sent to every Muslim province one copy of what they had
copied, and ordered that all the other Qur'anic materials
whether written in fragmentary manuscripts or whole copies
be burnt.[8]

There is disagreement between academics over the precise
details of the textual development of the Qur'an.[9] However,
scholars agree that the 'Uthmanic version of the Qur'an has
remained intact through to the present day.

Content of the Qur'an

Written in Arabic, the Qur'an consists of 114 chapters,
which are called Suras. These are arranged in order of
length (with some exceptions) rather than in the chronological order of revelation. Most of the longer Suras are
made up of sections which come from a variety of periods
in Muhammad's ministry. This makes precise dating of
each section rather difficult. Overall, eighty-six Suras were
given during the Meccan period and twenty-eight were
given in Medina. Each Sura other than Sura 9 begins with
the *bismillah* which is the statement "In the name of God,
the Mercy-giving, the Merciful". Each Sura is also given a
name which is derived from a theme or phrase which follows.

Literary Style

The Qur'an is written in Arabic poetry and prose and the
Islamic faith considers the very language of the Qur'an to be

totally unique. The book itself is held to be perfect, dictated by God and the ultimate expression of truth. The Iranian Islamic scholar Sayyid Hossein Nasr comments that:

> 'Many people, especially non-Muslims, who read the Qur'an for the first time are struck by what appears to be a kind of incoherence from the human point of view. It is neither like a high mystical text nor a manual of Aristotelian logic, though it contains both mysticism and logic.' He then goes on to say 'The Qur'an contains a quality which is difficult to express in modern language. One might call it divine magic.'[10]

Muslims believe that the Qur'an is the authenticating miracle of Islam. Whereas other prophets did miraculous deeds when Muhammad did none, the significant miracle of the Qur'an itself is what proves the superiority and finality of Islam.

Interpretation

Interpretation of the Qur'an is a complex issue within the worldwide and historical spectrum of Islam. A good starting place for understanding Islamic interpretation is the belief that any "translation" of the text from Arabic into another language robs the Qur'an of its divine authenticity. Any attempt to translate the Qur'an from Arabic is therefore seen merely as an interpretation and not a copy of the holy book itself. A number of specific schools of interpretation have developed over the centuries as Muslims wrestled with applying the text in their communities.[11] The Qur'an has increasingly been read through the lenses of these schools. Divisions between Muslims over what the Qur'an means have occurred when various sects have sought to abandon the interpretive framework laid down by centuries of scholars. Reforming movements have sought to get back to the "original" meaning of the text, unfettered by layers of human guidelines and traditions which had built up. Because of the inflammatory nature of some of the Suras of the Qur'an, these reforming groups have been inspired to take drastic action, which we will explore later in this book.

The Principle of Abrogation

One of the guiding principles of interpretation of the Qur'an is the principle of abrogation. This is absolutely crucial in negotiating some of the contradictions we find in the message. The message of the Qur'an was received over a period of 23 years and the principle of abrogation means that verses which come later take precedence over that which was given earlier. This is why pagan worship may be tolerated in early Meccan Suras but not later. It follows that earlier passages sympathetic to Christians and Jews are not taken so seriously as later condemnations. The later more fiery passages abrogate the earlier more tolerant passages. We read about this principle in the Qur'an itself in Sura 2:100: "And for whatever verse We abrogate or cast into oblivion, We bring a better or the like of it; knowest thou not that God is powerful over everything?"

The implications of this principle of abrogation are important if we are to understand the theological underpinnings of Islam. Muhammad became less tolerant of opposing views as his life went on and the passages quoted by violent Islamic groups such as Suras 8:40, 9:5, 9:14 and 9:125, do come later chronologically and therefore take precedence over the milder Suras.

The *Hadith* impact on the interpretation of the Qur'an very deeply. These extensive compilations provide an abundant reservoir of detail about the life of Muhammad, showing how Islam was lived out in its earliest era and providing instructions for those who seek to follow Muhammad as an example for their life. The *Hadith* are a companion to the Qur'an and are significant in helping to interpret the Muslim Scriptures. The *Hadith* are also the heartbeat of the legal and culture system of Muslims as the *Shariah* (shari'a) law is mostly derived from these ancient collections.

Themes of the Qur'an

The important themes of the Qur'an begin with the nature of God and the Oneness of Allah which we explored earlier. The

Qur'an deals with a whole range of theological themes and we will draw out the important ones here.

Eschatology

The Qur'an places significant emphasis on judgement and the afterlife"? One of Muhammad's most important tasks was to warn people about the Judgement of God. The picture painted is of hell as a place of torment and fire and heaven as a garden of bliss. The people in hell are in a fire (9:111), their scorched skins are exchanged for new ones so they can keep on suffering (4:59). Boiling water will be poured on them – melting their insides and skins (22:20) and people will be linked up together, unable to escape (69:30). Heaven on the other hand will involve sitting on majestic thrones and enjoying the attentions of beautiful virgins (37:40–50). There will be mansions and gardens, rivers and fountains (9:74). Both heaven and hell are spoken of with an emphasis on physical pleasure or torment. Unfortunately it is difficult to know to which destination one is headed. Muhammad initially included Christians and Jews in heaven: "Surely they that believe and those of Jewry and the Christians and the Sabeans whoso believes in God and the Last Day, and works righteousness – their wage awaits them with their Lord" (Sura 2:59). However this is abrogated by later verses which assure us that if one rejects the prophethood of Muhammad, hell will be the final destination (4:152, 5:84).

Even the Muslim is never assured of eternal salvation within Islam. On the contrary the Qu'ran is clear that it is impossible to know one's eternal destiny – each person will find their deeds weighed on scales at the end and only if the good outweighs the bad, will the person enter heaven (23:104–5). This ambiguity is a central theological plank of Islam and is absolutely crucial in understanding the rise of Islamic militancy and terrorism.

Other Holy Books

The Torah and the Gospels are declared by the Qur'an itself to be acceptable: "Say, O People of the Book! You have naught of guidance till you observe the Torah and the Gospel and that which was revealed unto you from your Lord" (5:68). In fact, Muhammad is himself commanded to look at these Scriptures when in doubt (10:94). However, historically, Muslims have claimed that the Gospels, known as the *Injil*, have been corrupted. Yusuf Ali comments that the *Injil* mentioned in the Qur'an is certainly not the New Testament and it is not the four Gospels as now received by the Christian Church, but an original Gospel which was promulgated by Jesus, as the Torah was promulgated by Moses and the Qur'an by Muhammad (Sura 2:86). Unfortunately there is simply no way of verifying that this is indeed the case. The Pentateuch and the four Gospels as we have them today were in existence during the time of Muhammad and for a long time before. Nowhere in the Qur'an is it stated that Christians, known as People of the Book, did not possess the authentic Scriptures and neither does the Qur'an itself claim that the *Injil* had been corrupted by Christians. The statement is made now because Muhammad's version of various biblical events differs from what we find in the texts of the Old and New Testaments. This is an important point because it is only later tradition which rejects the Bible, not the Qur'an itself.

Christ in the Qur'an

Jesus is a significant figure in the Qur'an; he is mentioned in 15 Suras and 93 verses speak of him. Islam speaks of Jesus with some honour in line with the other prophets but denies him the divine status recognized by the New Testament and the Christian Church. He is called by his proper name 'Isa and by the titles Messiah, Son of Mary, Messenger, Prophet, Servant, Word and Spirit of God. The Qur'an affirms the annunciation and virgin birth of Christ, and refers to his teachings, healings and exaltation. However, despite all of these titles much is made of emphasizing that Jesus is not what the Bible claims him to be. There are a number of passages in the Qu'ran denying that God has offspring. The Qur'an stresses the unity and oneness of God, denying his Trinitarian being and warning people against the divinity of Jesus Christ. Muhammad states in Sura 4:169 "O People of the Book, do not go beyond the bounds in your religion, and do not say anything about God but the truth. The Messiah Jesus, Son of Mary, is only a messenger from God."

One of the most fiercely defended aspects of Islamic thought about Jesus is the assertion that he did not really die on the cross. The Qur'an simply asserts that Jesus was not actually killed: "they did not slay him, neither crucified him, only a likeness of that was shown to them ... they slew him not of a certainty no indeed; God raised him up to Him" (Sura 4:156). There are many theories as to what happened; perhaps Simon of Cyrene, Judas or one of the disciples was substituted. Even though the idea of substitution has little foundation it is repeated today. Many Islamic scholars reject it, such as Dr Kamel Hussein: "The idea of a substitute for Christ is a very crude way of explaining the Qu'ranic text. They had to explain it to the masses. No cultured Muslim believes it nowadays." Whatever the nuances placed upon this text by different groups, the essence of the idea is that Jesus did not die on the cross, but was taken up to heaven by God miraculously. So Islam denies the sacrificial death of the saviour Jesus Christ and also denies his divinity.

Howevermuch Islam seeks to honour Jesus by giving him a position among the prophets, a virginal conception, numerous honoured titles, ascension into heaven and miraculous powers, this is a far cry from his New Testament status and the heart of the Christian faith. "For God was pleased to have all his fullness dwell in him, and through him to reconcile to himself all things whether things on earth or things in heaven, by making peace through his blood shed on the cross" (Col. 1:19–20). Interestingly, the *Encyclopaedia of Islam* (1981) suggests that "the closest analogue in Christian belief to the role of the Qur'an in Muslim belief is not the Bible, but Christ." Jesus himself is the eternal word. He is far superior to any book or text, he is God himself, coming in human form to live, die and be resurrected on this earth.

Judaism in the Qur'an

Initially Muhammad was sympathetic towards the Jews. In the early Meccan passages of the Qur'an he commends all People of the Book as he hoped that he would be accepted as their long-awaited prophet:

> Dispute not with the People of the Book save in the fairer manner, except for those of them that do wrong; and say, 'We believe in what has been sent down to us, and what has been sent down to you; and God and your God is One, and to Him we have surrendered' (Sura 29:45).

As time went past, the Arabian Jews and Christians increasingly rejected Muhammad and considered him to be a false prophet, and his growing frustration is reflected in the Qur'an. From his initially friendly comments Muhammad turns to condemnation of those who have rejected him as inauthentic: "Whoso desires another religion than Islam, it shall not be accepted of him; in the next world he shall be among the losers" (Sura 3:79–80). This attitude is not only reflected in his pronouncements about the afterlife but his words on earthly relationships between the different communities of People of the Book also turn sour. In Sura 9:29 the seeds of conflict against the Jews are sown:

> Fight those who believe not in God and the Last Day and do not forbid what God and His Messenger have forbidden – such men practise not the religion of truth, being of those who have been given the Book – until they pay the tribute out of hand and have been humbled.

The Qur'an explains this change of attitude towards the Jews in particular as a response to the rejection of prophets and messengers throughout history:

> So, for their breaking the compact, and disbelieving in the signs of God, and slaying the Prophets without the right, and for their

saying, 'Our hearts are uncircumcised' – nay, but God sealed them for their unbelief, so they believe not (Sura 4:154).

There are a wide range of themes raised in the Qur'an and further study of these could be usefully pursued at another time.[12]

The Rituals and Practice of Islam

The practice of Islam varies according to which sect a particular Muslim belongs to. There are quite a number of sects within Islam but the three most significant are introduced here:

● **Sunni** – Ninety per cent of all Muslims today are Sunnis and follow the *Sunna* (custom) about Muhammad that was passed on orally and finally written down in the *Hadith*. They accept the Qur'an literally.

● **Shi'ite** – Shi'ite Muslims follow Ali, who was Muh-ammad's cousin and the fourth caliph (chief ruler and successor of Muhammad) after Muhammad died. After Ali was murdered, his followers broke off from the main body of orthodox Islam. Shi'ites refuse to believe that God would leave Muslim leadership to the "vagaries of human election",[13] and they claim that God chose the house of Ali to lead the Islamic world. Most Shi'ite Muslims today live in Iran.

● **Sufi** – Sufism is an ascetic and mystic stream within Islam. Sufis seek to emulate Muhammad in his reception of ecstatic visions. Historically, renewal within Islam has sought to purge Sufi influences, but Sufism has survived as a mystical and at times persecuted group within the spectrum of Islam.

These different sects of Muslims all have subsections and significant breakaway sects within them. There is some animosity between these different communities, which has been expressed historically and still exists today.

Within these sects, however, the simple rituals remain broadly the same. For the person looking at a religion from the outside, the rituals are the most accessible characteristics to establish. Within classical Islam five "pillars", or actions, witness to the faith of the individual. Since their emergence in Islamic theological statements of the ninth century[14] the five pillars have been at the core of what it means to be a Muslim.

The practice of the five pillars of Islam should characterize each individual Muslim no matter where they live in the world.

Law

Another important facet of the practical outworking of Islam is the religious law. Islamic Law or *Shariah* comes from a number of different sources within Islam. The first is the Qu'ran – however, soon after the death of Muhammad it became apparent that the prescriptions of the Qu'ran were not enough for the shaping of a life or a community. Muhammad's followers began to collect narratives about the life and attitudes of their leader in various situations. These are recorded in the *Hadith* and principles for Law are drawn from the *Sunna* or "fine example" of Muhammad. The Qur'an and the *Hadith* are the principle sources for Islamic Law although Shi'ite Muslims will only accept *Hadith* traditions which can be traced back to Muhammad's son-in-law Ali and his descendants. It soon became apparent that passages from the Qur'an and *Hadith* allowed for different interpretations and were not altogether clear. Another authority was needed and so the *ijma* or "unanimous consensus" of a group of Muslim scholars was to be sought. The fourth and final source of Islamic law is found in the four schools of law which emerged as differences of opinion over various situations. These schools acknowledge each other and do not vary a great deal in their dogmas.

The *Shariah* legislation classifies behaviour into different categories. *Fard* are obligatory duties such as the five pillars, marriage, having children, providing for (male) and caring for (female) the family. *Halal* is that which is permitted – permitted food and drink, behaviour which is neutral, tolerated or recommended. *Haram* is that which is prohibited – behaviour or food which is forbidden except in life-threatening circumstances. The four schools do not always agree on the details of the practical implications of *fard*, *halal* and *haram* so that actual practice for the Muslim can depend quite heavily on which particular school is followed.

Islam teaches that the natural disposition of the human being is to err towards goodness and thus sin is an act which is against one's nature. Punishment is considered to be an integral part of the concept of justice. This does not mean that punishment is proportional to the crime or in any way atones for it; instead, punishment in Islam has a functional nature – it deters people from overstepping the boundaries of what is good and just and it is thus significant that punishments are called *hudud* which means boundaries. Punishments are liabilities incurred as a result of violating the limits set by God and are designed to keep alive the sense of justice in the community by public repudiation of such violations. Punishment is then limited to crimes mentioned in the Qur'an and *Hadith*, such as murder which is referred to in Sura 5:35.

The Friday Sermon

The *khutba* or Friday sermon is the weekly religious talk held every week at the noon prayers in a mosque. The preachers are to raise issues of concern for the local community and give an Islamic perspective, mediating between the big traditions of the religion and local events. The *khutba* is an important medium of expression bringing together the religious and the political in an applied and practical manner. Because of the influence of this role, Islamic regimes have increasingly curtailed the independence of the preachers, bringing them under the auspices of various state agencies.

Finances

Within Islam all wealth and possessions are to be seen as a gift from God. This is because all a person can do is invest labour in the process of production – it is God who makes it fruitful. Thus wealth is not to be spent only on oneself and one's family but it must also be used to help others who are in need or in distress: "and give the kinsman his right and the needy, and the traveller" (30:38). There are a number of mechanisms within Islam to help with the redistribution of wealth in a community. *Zakat* is one of the five pillars of Islam – every Muslim must pay 2.5% of their income to the poor. This is not an act of charity but an obligation in service to God. *Sadaqah* is a voluntary contribution – given by individuals over and above the necessary 2.5%. Voluntary contributions must be given in such a way that "even the left hand of the donor does not know what the right hand gives". Islam also prohibits giving and taking of interest on anything borrowed because this exploits those in need. "God blots out usury" (Sura 2:277). This makes for innovative economic policies in Islamic countries.

Islam means "surrender to God's will" or "submission" and a Muslim is one who submits. In Sura 1:5 Islam describes itself as "God's straight path" for the human race. It teaches that God has revealed his will - which is a path for people to follow so that they have guidance for every area of life. Right and wrong, good and bad are eternal unchangeable truths which God has revealed. The Qur'an, which is believed to be pure, divine revelation and the *sunna* recorded in the *Hadith* are the principal sources by which the Muslim can discern the moral way to live life. Every word of the Qur'an is believed to be the word of truth and its role must be understood as having wider implications than a sacred text because for the Muslim it is the first source of all knowledge and underpins every aspect of human existence. The *sunna* provide the second source of knowledge for the Muslim – the life of Muhammad is the living proof and example of the divine will and is a supply of knowledge for the Muslim on how to live in the world.

[1]   Anderson, *World Religions*, p. 95.

[2]   Haykal, Muhammad Husayn, *The Life of Muhammad*, p. 243–44.

[3]   In Schimmel, Annemarie, *And Muhammad is His Messenger*, p. 62.

[4]   Michael Nazir-Ali, *Frontiers in Muslim-Christian Encounter*, p. 133.

[5]   See Appendix.

[6]   In Jeffrey, Arthur, *Islam: Muhammad and His Religion*, p. 150.

[7]   Al-Bukhari, *The Translation of the Meaning of Sahih*, trans. Muhammad Muhshin Khan, vol. 6 pp. 477–78.

[8]   Ibid, pp. 478–79.

[9]   Discovery of some ancient Qur'anic fragments in Yemen in 1972 has led to increasing research of the textual development of the Qur'an. Puin is a specialist in Arabic calligraphy and Koranic paleography who is based at Saarland University, in Saarbrücken, Germany. He has been examining the Yemeni fragments since 1981. His findings reveal unconventional verse orderings, minor textual variations, and some artistic embellishment. Among the manuscripts some were palimpsests or versions which have clearly been written over even earlier, and then been washed off. What the Yemeni Qur'ans seemed to suggest, was an *evolving* text. Since the early 1980s more than 15,000 sheets of the Yemeni Qu'rans have painstakingly been flattened, cleaned, treated, sorted, and assembled; they now sit in Yemen's House of Manuscripts, awaiting detailed examination. In 1997 the task of taking more than 35,000 microfilm pictures of the fragments was finished and now scholars will be able to scrutinize the texts and to publish their findings freely. Andrew Rippon, Professor of Religious Studies at Calgary University, Canada, commented: "The impact of the Yemeni manuscripts is still to be felt.... Their variant readings and verse orders are all very significant. Everybody agrees on that. These manuscripts say that the early history of the Qur'anic text is much more of an open question than many have suspected: the text was less stable, and therefore had less authority, than has always been claimed." (January 1999 edition *Atlantic Monthly*)

[10]   Sayyid Hossein Nasr, *Ideals and Realities of Islam*, p. 47.

[11]   List of schools and dates ...

[12]   See Rippin, *Muslims*, vols 1&2, Kragg, *Islam from Within*.

[13]   Anderson, *Christianity*, p. 65.

[14] The five pillars appear in the *Hadith* collections of al-Bukhari (d.870) and Muslim ibn al-Hajjaj (d.875).

2

Extreme Islam

The emergence of the Taliban movement in Afghanistan, as well as numerous other terrorist networks around the world, has catapulted Islamic extremism into the headlines. The events of 11 September 2001 – the destruction of both the World Trade Center and a section of the Pentagon in the United States – have become iconic representations of a militant Islamic world-view. We have witnessed the powerful clash of global symbolism: the targets chosen represented American dominance of global capitalism and military might, and the use of American airlines to bring destruction showed the ability of terrorists to work within the Western system, and exploit its inherent weaknesses. It is because September 11th combines the reality of human tragedy with symbolic significance that this type of Islamic terrorism has the ability both to confuse and to frighten the wider community. What is the explanation for this stream of militant Islam?

Fundamentalism

A brief discussion of definitions of the term "fundamentalism" is important because use of the word ranges from the technical to the pejorative. Historically, fundamentalism finds its roots within Protestantism in America and Britain in the late nineteenth century, especially among Brethren and Baptist denominations, and must be seen to be working alongside other theological streams such as Dispensationalism, Pentecostalism and the Holiness Movement, which arose from the same era, and came to prominence in the 1920s[1] After this time "fundamentalism" became a descriptive label that was used more widely, and since the 1970s, increasingly has been used to denote movements and theologies in other faith communities, particularly in Islam. Even in the contemporary era there is a noticeable disparity from one side of the Atlantic to the other. In America, "fundamentalism" still retains the initially positive meaning in some church circles of "holding to the fundamentally important" principles and aspects of the faith; whereas in Europe, it is doubtful whether "fundamentalism" could really be used in a non-pejorative sense outside the confines of academic theology.

Where sensitive scholarship has attempted to clarify fundamentalism it has been defined simply as "*the belief in old traditional forms of religion, or the belief that what is written in a holy book is completely true*".[2] The majority of the adherents of all the major world religions would be "fundamentalist" if this catch-all understanding is maintained. This definition is in danger also of anachronism, for there would be little to differentiate a traditional, pre-Enlightenment approach to the scriptures from a fundamentalist one.

Another explanation of what is meant by "fundamentalism" is a development of the first, but places it more firmly in the modern era, calling fundamentalism:

> a usually religious movement or point of view characterized by a return to fundamental principles, by rigid adherence to those principles and often by intolerance of other views and opposition to secularism.[3]

Here fundamentalism is described with reference to both its creative and resistant elements. Creatively it involves a return to fundamental principles, in a context where the believing community seems to have disregarded them, and then a tenacious allegiance to those principles once they have been established. This, it is then argued, cannot be expressed without resisting what is perceived to be its opposites in other ideologies and expressly in secularism. Thus it follows that the key to fundamentalism is not the intolerant stance taken, but the principles decided upon in the first place.

However, since the 1950s, before "fundamentalism" was regularly used descriptively of non-Christian ideologies or religions, it had already become necessary for many religious conservatives, particularly in Britain, to emphasize the distinctiveness of Fundamentalism and show the wider public that Evangelicalism and Fundamentalism were not synonymous. This was the era of Billy Graham's first Mission to England, by which time Fundamentalism was well entrenched as a derogatory term in the media to describe religious obscurantism and extremism. John Stott and J.I. Packer were among those who entered into this debate stressing that while Evangelicals affirmed the complete truth of the Christian Scriptures and their supreme authority for matters of doctrine and conduct, they also acknowledged a scope for differing interpretation among those who accept this view of Scripture. However, in contemporary scholarship, particularly among those less sympathetic to the evangelical view of Scripture, many prefer the inclusive stance of James Barr:

> Although logically fundamentalism is only one circle within the several that constitute evangelicalism ... numerically it is much the most populous: let's say, something well over ninety per cent of world evangelicalism is fundamentalist, and, even for many of those not included in that percentage fundamentalism commonly remains the ideological standard by which it is determined what is evangelical and what is conservative.[4]

What is plain, however, is that there are two definite nuances to the word "fundamentalism". The first is broad and encompasses movements within all religious and ideological groupings which resist "modernism" and maintain or demand the absolute trustworthiness of their texts. The second has a more technical and restricted use mainly in the United States. It is probable that the extension of the term "fundamentalism" to a broad spectrum

of movements from within Islam and other world religions is
due partly to the Iranian revolution, which catapulted the emergence of radical Islamic forms of theology into the global political arena. Both the rejection of "Westernization" and the
reliance on the Qur'an reminded observers of religious tendencies within some Christian groups.

Defining fundamentalism, even within Islam alone, is
notoriously difficult. William Shepard distinguishes between
the emergent streams of Islam contrasting "fundamentalism"
with the three other orientations, which may be labelled
"traditionalist", "secularist" and "modernist". He writes:

> The traditionalists or conservatives are those who have resisted
> the Westernizing tendencies of the last century or two in the name
> of Islam as understood and practised in particular areas, and have
> been found particularly among … the Sufi orders, and generally
> among the rural populations and lower classes.[5]

Examples of these include the nineteenth-century Sufi brother-
hoods of Nigeria:

> The secularists are those who have sought to clear the way for
> social reform by restricting religion to personal devotion and
> ritual (and possibly family law) and asserted the authority of 'rea-
> son' in public life, usually guided by Western precedents and
> Western-derived ideologies, especially nationalism.[6]

This can broadly be equated with the stance taken by the
Turkish government, and the earlier expressions of Pakistan's
legislature.

> By contrast, modernists have insisted that Islam is relevant to all
> areas of life, public as well as private, but that the traditional views
> and practices must be reformed in the light of the original sources
> of authority, the Qur'an and the Sunnah and of contemporary con-
> ditions and needs. For modernists the shariah applies to all of life,
> but they tend to emphasis its flexibility and tend in practice to
> interpret it in terms of Western-derived ideas.[7]

This approach to Islam has been the dominant response to the more "liberal" elements within the Islamic community living in the West.

> 'Fundamentalists' also want to interpret Islam in terms of original sources of authority in the light of contemporary needs, but they strongly object to the modernists' tendency to 'Westernize' Islam. For them the shariah is indeed flexible and capable of development to meet changing need, but interpretation and development must be done in a genuinely Islamic manner, and must not involve covert forms of Westernizing. They also criticize many of the traditional ways and practices, but even more they object to the tendency of many traditionalists to tolerate and even co-operate with secularizing governments in practise.[8]

A similar conclusion is drawn on the definition of fundamentalism by Oliver Roy, in his book *The Failure of Political Islam*. He characterizes political Islam as being in keeping with two pre-existing Islamic tendencies: "One ... is the call to fundamentalism, centred on the Sharia: this call is as old as Islam itself and is yet still new because it has never been fulfilled." He explains "fundamentalism" as being reform which censors corruption and moral laxity and re-emphasizes sacred texts. The second tendency "is that of anti-colonialism, of anti-imperialism, which today has simply become 'anti-Westernism'."[9]

"Islamism" is thus seen as the enemy among more liberal expressions of Islam, for both sides want to win the battle for legitimacy and orthodoxy in the public sphere. This is also true of Islamic discourse *within* and *with* the West. Even among emerging "fundamentalist" groups there is also competition for the right to interpret afresh, and this can lead to greater radicalism and extremism.[10]

Islamisms

It may be clearer by now that "fundamentalism" is a catch-all term, which, though popular in the media, has been resisted in

more recent years by scholars of Islamic thought.[11] The desire
for a resurgent Islamic society and political system is fairly
universal, but the militant, or as we will now term them,
"Islamist", groups have certain convictions about how the
Islamic rebirth might best be achieved. Daniel Pipes defines
Islamism as:

> an ideology that demands man's complete adherence to the sacred
> law of Islam and rejects as much as possible outside influence,
> with some exceptions (such as access to military and medical tech-
> nology). It is imbued with a deep antagonism toward non-
> Muslims and has a particular hostility toward the West. It amounts
> to an effort to turn Islam, a religion and civilization, into an ideol-
> ogy.[12]

One can recognize a gentle chronological pattern across the
Islamic world: during the sixties to early eighties the top-
down model of Islamization prevailed among more radical
groups. Revolution and the toppling of tyrants were seen as
the best way of achieving Islamic renewal of society, along the
lines of the Iranian revolutionary model. This former mecha-
nism of change gave way in the eighties to movements that
concentrated on "Islamic spaces", a bottom-up approach that
would begin to affect the rest of society. This latter was
demonstrated through the Taliban, who established a sense of
Islamic rule and society in the Kandahar region, and extended
their model of Islamic society throughout the rest of the
nation. When we interviewed them it was the sense of building a model Islamic society to be copied in other nations,
which seemed (at least in their "articulated" intentions) to be
inspiring them.

A militant group within the sphere of worldwide Islam can
be characterized by a desire to accept the technological and
cultural challenges of modernity in a controlled fashion –
using the authoritative sources of Islam to monitor change in
the present. This is why Islamist groups are happy to use
certain technologies, especially in weapons, travel and communications, to further their cause. Islamism also emphasizes

the pan-Islamic over nationalism, which is why the Islamist terrorist networks traverse national boundaries, and respond readily to the call to *jihad* wherever that might be. One author has set out the following characteristics of emergent groups within Islam as having:

a) a deep transforming concern with the socio-moral degeneration of Muslim society;
b) a call to go back to original Islam and shed the superstitions inculcated by popular forms of Sufism, to get rid of the idea of the finality of the traditional schools of law, and to attempt to rethink for oneself the meaning of the original message;
c) a call to remove the crushing burden of a deterministic outlook produced by popular religion;
d) a call to carry out this revivalist reform through armed force *jihad* if necessary.[15]

Such is the platform that several movements in contemporary Islam have inherited. One can see that many of these intentions are constructive, hopeful and pious and are as much a declaration of intent for the revival of vibrant Islam as they are a cry of resistance against ideologies that seem to undermine the faith.

It may be surprising to some that these emergent groups within Islam are not always economically and intellectually disadvantaged.[16] Daniel Pipes comments: "I also wish to note that Islamism has few connections to wealth or poverty; it is not a response to deprivation. There is no discernible connection between income and Islamism."[17] Fat'hi ash-Shiqaqi, a well-educated young Palestinian living in Damascus, had a love for European literature – he had read and enjoyed Shakespeare, Dostoyevsky, Chekhov, Sartre and Eliot. He had a particular passion for Sophocles' *Oedipus Rex*, a work he read ten times in the English translation "and each time wept bitterly".[18] Exposure and sensitivity to world literature in a man assassinated as the head of the *Islamic Jihad*, an arch-terrorist organization, is perhaps surprising. But

Shiqaqi's familiarity with things Western fits a common pattern. Hasan at-Turabi, the effective ruler of Sudan, is the man behind the brutal persecution of his country's large Christian minority. He has an intimate knowledge of the West and claims that most militant Islamic leaders, like himself, are "from the Christian, Western culture. We speak your languages."[19]

This pattern points to a paradox: the very people intent on radicalizing the Muslim world have been exposed to, and appreciate certain aspects of, Western culture, while simultaneously demonizing other aspects, especially morality and dress. Their Islamic militancy is seldom born of ignorance and poverty, but is rather an informed response to what has been seen and experienced.

Theology

Despite issues of poverty and politics which provoke and inspire radical adherents within the theologies of Islam, the underlying debate is one of interpretation, particularly interpretation of the Qur'an and the Sunnah in the light of contemporary beliefs and practices.[20] Islamisms must be seen, in part, as theological responses to the struggle for authoritative interpretation. This competition for supremacy among Muslim leaders has increased since the abolition of the unifying Caliphate in 1924.[21]

As we focus on Islamic extremism the potent issue of interpreting the Qur'an and the *Hadith* arises. The nature of scripture itself is not at stake, as virtually all Muslims hold the Qur'an to be the verbatim word of God, a view we explored in the first chapter. However, there are various theological ideas within the Qur'an which have become characteristic of Islamism. Two theological concepts in particular have been picked up by the media: namely Holy War, or *jihad*, and martyrdom, or *shahid*. The Qur'anic inspiration for Islamist movements cannot be ignored. The political, economic and social factors in the development of extreme groups are important and frequently analyzed. However, the self-proclaimed inspiration of Islamist groups is expressly Qur'anic and theological. Where do these ideas come from, and why have they gained such potency?

Jihad

The word *jihad* is derived from the verb *jahada*, which means "he exerted himself" or "he strove". Literally, then, *jihad* means striving – exerting oneself in contending against an enemy. *Jihad* also conveys the concept of an individual's private struggle against evil at a personal level. Waging war against the carnal soul, "the inner struggle", is an important part of *jihad*. Ibn Qaiyim al-Djawziya, a noted thirteenth-century scholar, asserts: "The *jihad* against the enemies of Allah with one's life is only part of the struggle which a true servant of Allah carries on against his own self for the sake of the Lord."[22] But in its most outward and public form the *jihad* has been used by Muslims through the ages to make war sacred. *Jihad* is fighting in the way of God – holy war.

> 'Slay the idolaters wherever you find them, and take them, and confine them, and lie in wait for them at every place of ambush. But if they repent, and perform the prayer, and pay the alms, then let them go their way,' says the Qur'an (Sura 9:5).

An explanatory note in the respected translation by A. Yusuf Ali makes clear that this is not intended metaphorically: "When war becomes inevitable it must be pursued with vigour. The fighting may take the form of slaughter, or capture, or siege, or ambush and other stratagems."[23]

There are some Muslims who argue that this verse need not be interpreted literally any more, but many do still hold that the Qur'an is the immutable word of God and that these sections have enduring practical relevance. It is true that the Qur'an also contains verses urging tolerance of non-Muslims, as we have seen, but these verses frequently pre-date the more belligerent ones and are thus abrogated by them.[24] Another verse from the Qur'an says:

You shall be called against a people possessed of great might to fight them, or they surrender. If you obey, God will give you a goodly wage; but if you turn your back, as you turned your backs before, He will chastise you with a painful chastisement (Sura 48:16).

The meaning here is that Muslims should fight until their opponents embrace Islam. In the early days of Islam, the faith was indeed spread by the sword. Those who would not embrace Islam were killed. Such instances are recorded in the *Hadith*: "Allah's Apostle said, 'The Hour will not be established until you fight with the Jews, and the stone behind which a Jew will be hiding will say. "O Muslim! There is a Jew hiding behind me, so kill him."'"[25] Another incident recorded in the *Hadith* tells a similar story:

> While we were in the Mosque, the Prophet came out and said, 'Let us go to the Jews.' We went out till we reached Bait-ul-Midras. He said to them, 'If you embrace Islam, you will be safe. You should know that the earth belongs to Allah and His Apostle, and I want to expel you from this land. So, if anyone among you owns some property, he is permitted to sell it, otherwise you should know that the Earth belongs to Allah and His Apostle.'[26]

This approach has been emulated across the world in our own era. In Indonesia, for example, at least 7,000 people were forcibly converted to Islam by well-armed Islamic extremists during the 1990s. Those who refused were killed.[27]

Both modern and traditional Islamic scholars have treated *jihad* in the context of military action as the only form of justifiable war. *Jihad* is thus an instrument of Islamic mission and, if necessary, can be used for the defence of Islam. It is in this military sense that *jihad* is most commonly referred to in the Qur'an and *Hadith* – an armed struggle used as an instrument to establish or defend Islamic social order.

Martyrdom

The sense of *jihad* as armed struggle for the sake of God encompasses the theological idea of *shahid* – martyrdom in the process of fighting for God. *Shahid* literally means "the one who has testified", and carries with it a sense of witness. The *shahid* is one who has testified to his faith upon the battlefield, and he is promised that he will in turn witness God (4:70). The Qur'an assures Muslims that martyrs will be shown favour. If someone has been slain in the way of God he will experience joy, bounty and blessing (3:164) and can expect to pass into paradise with certainty, avoiding the punishment of the grave. In a religion that is generally ambiguous about who will be saved[28] this theological certainty is incredibly attractive. For the zealous Muslim who is yearning for heaven and not hell, there is no certainty that good deeds will outweigh bad on the day of judgement. Only martyrdom in a *jihad* can promise this elusive assurance.

In a cultural context of young men volunteering for suicide missions, the ideological and theological premises for their actions must be taken seriously. Much has been made of the poverty and hopelessness these Muslim men face, and of their sense of being politically disenfranchised in the increasingly globalized context of the late twentieth and early twenty-first centuries. However, many of those who offer themselves for suicide missions are in fact university educated and have good economic prospects. We cannot, therefore, underestimate the theological motivation behind these martyrdoms. For extremely zealous individuals searching for assurance of salvation from the God they serve an attractive option, giving a sense of purpose and destiny, is martyrdom.

History

The Life of Muhammad

As we begin to look at the origins of violence and armed struggle within Islam we find that the founder of the faith himself came to a point at which he began to sanction violence. When Muhammad first started to preach his religion of Islam, he was not violent. We have seen that many of the early Meccan passages of the Qur'an show a certain sympathy for non-Muslims. The *Hadith* tell us, however, that just before leaving for Medina Muhammad believed that he received a revelation allowing him to fight the Meccans.[29]After moving to Medina, Muhammad fell into conflict with the Arabian Jews and pagans in the area. Again, the *Hadith* give us various renditions of the events: "The Apostle of Allah said: If you gain a victory over the men of the Jews, kill them. So Muhayyisah jumped over Shubaybah, a man of the Jewish merchants. He had close relations with them. He killed him."[30] One Islamic scholar sums up the incredulity with which such acts have been met: "It is remarkable that tradition attributes Muhammad's most cruel acts to divine order, namely the siege of Qaynuqa, the murder of Kab, and the attack upon Qurayzah."[31]

Another incident narrated in the *Hadith* tells of the author hearing Muhammad say: "I will expel the Jews and Christians from the Arabian Peninsula and will not leave any but Muslim."[32] The contemporary Muslim scholar Ali Dashti, commenting on the life of Muhammad, observed that in the very earliest period Islam mutated into a violent force: "Thus Islam was gradually transformed from a purely spiritual mission into a militant and punitive organization whose progress depended on booty from raids and revenue from zakat tax."[33]

Radical Islamic Movements

Violent expressions of Islam have a rich ideological history within the religion. The Assassins were an Islamic sect dating from the eleventh to the thirteenth centuries and were renown for murdering their enemies as a religious duty. The group got their name from the Arabic *hashshash*, meaning "hashish smoker" – referring to their practice of taking hashish to induce ecstatic visions of paradise before their own martyrdoms. The group was a product of political rivalries within the Shi'ite leadership. Hasan-e-Sabbah and others refused to recognize the new Caliph in Cairo and transferred their allegiance to his brother. In 1090, Hasan and his allies captured the hill fortresses of Alamut in Iran, where he set up his headquarters. By the end of the eleventh century Hasan commanded a chain of strongholds all over Iran and Iraq – the Assassins – a network of propagandists and terrorists devoted to his cause.

Ibn Taymiyya, who died in 1328, is one of the intellectual heroes of radical Islam. He argued for purifying Islam from various practices prevalent at his time such as tomb visitations and the worship of saints. His argument against these things appealed for a return both to the Qur'an and to the *Sunna* of Muhammad. He asserted that anything that could not be justified based on these sources was to be rejected. On this basis, music and song were considered non-Islamic – an idea that was picked up and expressed by the Taliban. A similar thinker named Ibn Abd al-Wahhab (1703-87) also encouraged single-minded reliance on Islamic texts. The movements connected to Ibn Abd al-Wahhab and to Shah Wali Allah may be called "purification movements". They provide precedents in Islamic history for violent reforming Islamist groups. Such movements are not innovations of the twentieth century.

The Contemporary Era

In more recent times many Islamist movements have emerged around the world. One of the most influential groups which most clearly articulated the theological and practical methods of reform was the Muslim Brotherhood. In 1928, Hasan al-Banna founded the Society of Muslim Brethren (the Muslim Brotherhood) in Egypt. Al-Banna was concerned to see a revival of Islam in Egypt based on a strict adherence to the Qur'an:

> You are not a benevolent organization, nor a political party, nor a local association with limited aims. Rather you are a new spirit making its way to the heart of the nation, and reviving it through the Qur'an: a new light dawning and scattering the darkness of materialism through the knowledge of God. You are a resounding voice rising and echoing the message of the Apostle.[34]

According to al-Banna, the Islamic way of life, or the call (*da 'wa*) is an evolutionary process that begins with the reform of the individual and ends with the supremacy of Islam in the world.

> Thus the da'wa proceeds in stages, from the forming of the Muslim home, though directing the society and liberating the country from what is un-Islamic, to the building of an international status for the Islamic Community (Umma). In this scheme ... the violent form of jihad only comes as the last resort and under the specific conditions of colonialism.[35]

Up until 1952, successive Egyptian governments did not seek to impede the preaching of al-Banna and his followers as they proclaimed their hatred of British colonialism and their contempt for Westernized elites. All this changed in 1952 under President Nasser, when the state decked itself in the colours of "Arab socialism" and any critic of this either remained silent or was imprisoned. When al-Banna died in February 1949 it was, in the words of R. Mitchell, "a tragedy of incalculable proportions"[36] for the Muslim Brotherhood. Although a successor was found in Hasan al-Hudaybi, he never really filled the void left by al-Banna. Instead, a Muslim Brother called Sayyid Qutb filled this vacuum.

On 26 October 1954, a Muslim Brother called Mahmud al-Latif tried to assassinate President Nasser in Alexandria's Menshieu Square. This action expressed the opposition of the Brotherhood to Nasser's totalitarian state and the fact that Egypt had become the "United Arab Republic". Many of the Brothers were arrested, including Sayyid Qutb, and it was from his concentration camp that Qutb wrote the famous book *Signposts*. In this work Qutb calls for an Islamic revival and refers to his own society as *jahiliyya* (a Qur'anic term for the pre-Islamic unbelievers). This was a unique assertion on the part of Qutb, for al-Banna himself had never denounced Egypt as being *jahiliyya*. Qutb writes: "How must this Islamic resurrection begin? A vanguard must resolve to set it in motion in the midst of the *jahiliyya* that now reigns over the entire earth

... it is for this long-awaited vanguard that I have written *Signposts*."[37]

Qutb argues that if it is true that contemporary society has been reduced to pre-Islamic *jahiliyya*, Muslims must view society as the Prophet and his companions viewed their own society. Muhammad emigrated from Mecca to Medina on a journey known as the Hijra, when he was in a weak position, only to return to Mecca as a military and political conqueror. According to Qutb, the process by which *jahiliyya* society can be destroyed and a Muslim state erected is *jihad*: "... the battle is constant, and the sacred combat (*jihad*) lasts until Judgment Day".[38] The concept of *jihad* is explained in a chapter of *Signposts* called *al-jihad fi sabil allah*, "The Sacred Combat in the Path of God", where Qutb argues against the softening of *jihad* by "defeatists" who limit it to "defensive war" or confine it to the solitary inner combat of the believer against temptation. For Qutb, *jihad* is a weapon by which the Muslim may free himself from the yoke of oppression. This concurs with al-Banna, who explained the importance of *jihad* for the Muslim Brotherhood of Egypt in this way: "How wise was the man who said that 'force is the surest way of implementing the right' and how beautiful it is that force and right should march side by side."[39]

Qutb was briefly released from imprisonment in 1964, but he was soon arrested again and sentenced to death under suspicion of reforming the Brotherhood with the intention of a renewed armed struggle.

In November 1977, President Anwar Sadat of Egypt travelled to Jerusalem on a mission for peace in the Middle East. His independent gesture, an attempt to end the hatred and violence between the Arabs and the Israelis, was interpreted as betrayal – because with his trip Sadat broke a 29-year Arab ban on direct dealings with the Israelis. The ban had existed since the founding of the State of Israel in 1948. Consequently, Sadat's statement to Israel's Knesset: "to live with you in permanent peace and justice" became well known around the world.

Until President Sadat's initiative, a political deadlock of three decades had been firmly established. The peace process bore its first fruit in 1979, when the leaders of Egypt, the United States and Israel all signed a formal treaty. For the first time in 31 years, Egypt and Israel were no longer at war. As a result, however, President Sadat (himself a Muslim) was assassinated on 6 October 1981 by Islamic extremists. The accomplices are believed to have been from an extremist splinter group of the Muslim Brotherhood of Egypt.

Shukri Ahmed Mustafa, a leader of an extreme group of Muslim brethren who was accused of the murder of the Egyptian Trusts and Bequests Minister, said that the movement's philosophy was based on "sacred hatred" of current liberal Islamic trends which he believed had departed from the true faith. Before he was hanged in 1978, he said that spilling the blood of heretics is the sacred duty of all Muslims. It seems that the assassination of President Sadat was part of an established pattern of attempts to stimulate an Islamic revolution that would lead to the foundation of the Islamic Republic of Egypt.

However, the theological and socio-political influence of the Islamic Brotherhood of Egypt is hard to overemphasize. For although tangible, direct influence is scarce, they have been influential in laying the foundations of Islamic extremism as a theological model to be emulated or adapted in nearly every nation in the world that has a significant Muslim population. The brotherhood were in fact less extreme than movements such as Islamic Jihad in Palestine, but their perceived moderation inspired other groups to express a more "radical" political or military stance in order to achieve their aims. Qutb's theological restatement of da'wa has been picked up in other countries, and greatly influences contemporary interpretation of the Qur'an, especially where strict Islam is a minority. Piscatori writes:

> From the perspective of the fundamentalist, the stakes are high: the faith must be protected from assault and preserved from heterodoxy. Da'wa in Iraq says the elimination of Saddam "the enemy of religion and the Qur'an" is the pre-eminent duty of every Muslim, and according to Islamic Jihad in the West Bank and

Gaza, one obeys either 'God and his Prophet' or ... the Israeli occupiers.[40]

Mubarak's Egypt becomes *dar-al-kuft* (land of unbelief), Saddam's Iraq is *jahili* (pre-Islamic pagan) society, and Israel the descendant of treacherous Jews of the prophetic time depicted in the Qur'an.[41]

To Sum Up

The principles of "pure Islam" and using *jihad* as a means of bringing about political change in an Islamic country are essential bases for an Islamist movement. However, the Taliban is unique when compared to other movements within Islam, because of their lack of intellectual sophistication. This fact, as well as their isolation from other Muslims, makes them an interesting case study. If they are not so deeply influenced by the ideology of other militant movements and their response to modernism and if they have had little or no exposure to Western culture, where do their ideas come from? When interviewing the Taliban in 1996 we asked this question, and the reply was always the same: "The Qur'an." The Taliban were happy to use sophisticated technology to advance their aims, but their own ideology is a simple attempt at the moral and spiritual reformation of Afghanistan based on the Qur'an and *Shariah*. They see themselves as a pure, simple, rustic expression of true Islam. The Taliban do fit loosely within a worldwide stream of Islamism – in fact they have inspired and galvanized a new breed of Islamic extremism who have sympathizers in nearly every nation. The Taliban's initial lack of exposure to influences outside of Pakistan and Afghanistan meant that their ideas come from the texts they hold dear and from their own culture.

The Taliban offer the world a new expression of Sunni Islamism, which had succeeded in taking over a whole nation. Islamic reform was initiated, sponsored and forcibly imposed on a Muslim population by the state. This new kind of extremism rejects any contact with Muslim moderation or Western culture, while accepting much Western technology. The Taliban openly refused to negotiate with the UN and other humanitarian aid agencies and rejected all attempts to compromise their principles in order to achieve wider international acceptance. Their belief in the inherent corruption of all moderate Muslim rulers has inspired a whole generation of young militants – the terrorist training camps were overwhelmed with idealistic recruits. The new face of extreme Islam cannot be called fundamentalist in the general sense; it bears no similarity to fundamentalist Protestant responses to modernism. Rather, the Taliban have expressed Islam in a way that is single-minded in its commitment and refusal to compromise with other Muslims – let alone the West. This generation of extremists is passionately committed to their cause. They find meaning, purpose and assurance in their religious zeal and even in their own death for the cause.

There have always been followers within Islam who have taken the words of the Qur'an as their motivation for violent *jihad*. And while there have always been some social, political and economic explanations for this violence, we cannot ignore the theological motivation that has been expressed by generation after generation of Muslims: the desire to follow the original teachings and ethics of the Qur'an and Muhammad.

---

[1] Harris, H, *Fundamentalism and Evangelicals*, for further reading.

[2] *The Cambridge International Dictionary of English*.

[3] Dictionary.com.

[4] Barr, *Fundamentalism and Evangelical Scholarship*, p.144. Barr's thesis is untenable for a host of reasons, but in our opinion, primarily because it is so firmly rejected by the Evangelical Alliance, and by nearly all those who understand themselves to be Evangelical in Britain. Harris, *Fundamentalism and Evangelicals*, p. 1–11 explores this Evangelical self-understanding, though Harris largely supports Barr's thesis.

[5] Shepard, *Fundamentalism*, p. 258. Also *Comments*, p. 282.

[6] Ibid.

[7]   Ibid.

[8]   Ibid.

[9]   Roy, *The Failure of Political Islam*, p. 3.

[10] Auda, Gehad, *Normalisation of the Islamic Movement in Egypt*, p. 364.

[11] We have expressed it plurally here (Islamisms) in keeping with the analysis of J.F. Legrain (*Palestinian Islamisms*, p. 413) who argues that the singular (Islamism) is "too monolithic, and easily categorized". In this article is also traced the "chronological analysis" of Kepel and Roy.

[12] Pipes, Daniel, *Distinguishing between Islam and Islamism,* Center for Strategic and International Studies, June 30, 1998.

[15] Rahman, *Islam: Challenges and Opportunities*, p. 317.

[16] Legrain, J.F, *Palestinian Islamisms*, p.414–416. Shows the importance of charitable organizations and schools, and shows how Fatah emphasized its ability to tackle poverty, not just reflect it.

[17] Pipes, Internet article.

[18] Pipes, *The Western Mind of Radical Islam*, pp. 18–23.

[19] Pipes, *Western Mind*, pp. 18-23.

[20] See Roberts, Hugh, *Algerian Islamism*, p. 478.

[21] Piscatori, *Accounting for Islamic Fundamentalisms*, p. 365.

[22] Cited in A.H. Siddiqi, *Jihad in Islam: A Comprehensive View*, p. 28.

[23] Yusaf Ali on Surah 9:5.

[24] Abrogation: see Chapter 1.

[25] Sunan of Abu Huraira, Vol. 4, Bk. 52, No. 177.

[26] Sunan of Abu Huraira. Vol. 4, Bk. 53, No. 392.

[27] The strong words of President Wahid, himself a Muslim, reflected his alarm that the campaign of Christian genocide which had been waged for the past eight months in the remote provinces of Maluku and North Maluku was now being deliberately spread throughout his vast country. "Their steps are to destablise the government and create fear and panic," he stated. The extremists intend the elimination of Christians from the Malukus to be simply the first stage of their overall plan, which is to eradicate Christians and Christianity from the whole of Indonesia and make it an Islamic state governed by Shari'ah (Islamic law). At least 5,000 (probably many more) have been killed in the past two years, and an estimated 487,000 have been forced to flee their homes. Some 7,000 have been forcibly converted

to Islam. At least 455 church buildings have been destroyed, as well as countless thousands of Christian homes, shops and a Christian university. "Moderate Muslims and Christians have demonstrated in Jakarta, calling for urgent intervention in the Moluccas by UN peacekeepers. They argue that what is happening in the Moluccas is nothing short of religious and cultural genocide." Edward Leigh MP, 19 December 2000.

http://www.barnabasfund.org/Indonesia%20petition/Indonesia_2000.htm

[28] See Ch. 1 section on Eschatology.

[29] Guillaume, *The Life of Muhammad*. See again, Ch. 1 for an outline for the chronology of Muhammad's life.

[30] Sunan of Abu Dawud, Bk. 19, No. 2996.

[31] Wensinck, *Muhammad and the Jews of Medina*, p. 113.

[32] 'Umar b. al-Khattib, Bk. 019, No. 4366.

[33] Dashti, *23 Years: A Study of the Prophetic Career of Muhammad*, p. 100.

[34] Adly, *'Contours of Islamic Theology'* (article).

[35] Auda, Gehad, *The Normalisation of Islam in Egypt*. p. 377.

[36] Mitchell, *The Society of the Muslim Brothers*, p. 299.

[37] Qutb, *Signposts*, p. 12.

[38] Qutb, *Signposts*, p. 130.

[39] Adly, *Contours of Islamic Theology*."

[40] Piscatori, J, *Accounting for Islamic fundamentalisms*, p. 635.

[41] Sura VII, 166; Sura III, 14.

3

Afghanistan's Taliban: An Example of Islamism

Different movements around the Islamic world, who subscribe to literalist and extremist interpretations of the Qur'an, are increasingly engaged in military and terrorist activities. Within the broad spectrum of the Islamic faith there are a number of vocal and highly publicized radical movements which are gaining momentum. One particular case of a radical Islamist group which caught the world's attention was the Taliban movement in Afghanistan. The Taliban have become incredibly influential on an international level, contributing trained fighters and zealous Islamist ideals to political causes in Islamic countries and beyond. In this chapter we will explore the conditions in which this movement emerged and evaluate the importance of religious ideals in relation to political and cultural factors.

Talib means "student of religion" in Pashtu, hence the name "Taliban" was taken up by the radical Sunni Islamic movement, which rose up in Afghanistan in 1996. One might expect a movement called "students of religion" to be made up of young students – this was however not strictly the case with Afghanistan's Taliban. Although there were indeed many young men among the Taliban foot soldiers, the name Taliban indicates the origins of the movement more accurately than what it went on to become.

The Taliban originate from the Pashtu people group and the movement emerged from among the tribal Pashtus who straddle the rural Afghan-Pakistan border. Less than half of the indigenous population of Afghanistan is ethnically Pashtu.[1] The Taliban subscribed passionately to the basic tenets of cultural Pashtu characteristics – honour, revenge and respect for private property. It has been argued by some that the Taliban had less to do with Qur'anic interpretation than with Pashtu culture.[2]

The movement can be clearly traced back to the "Madrassahs" or "religious schools" which operate in the north of Pakistan. In these schools the Qur'an is the centre of all teaching and boys aged from twelve to sixteen years old learn the Qur'an off by heart in Arabic. The extreme form of Islam taught in such schools is narrow and the curriculum predominantly consists of reciting the Qur'an, with other subjects being touched upon only superficially. The Madrassah system has been nurtured by years of poverty and illiteracy; this is partly because a family who send a son will not have to feed or clothe him – not only this but they are also considered blessed by Allah for giving up a child to spread the teachings of the Prophet. The Madrassahs have a poor human rights record and the Pakistan Human Rights Agency has released reports that children are frequently put in leg irons to prevent them from escaping. Perhaps one of the most influential teachings of the Madrassahs is their espousal of the role of *jihad* meaning "struggle" or in the popular parlance of some Muslims "holy war" in the political and religious life of a Muslim.

The Madrassahs in Pakistan from which the Taliban emerged were heavily influenced by the *deobandi* a political movement in Pakistan administered by traditionalists and reformist 'ulamas who dedicated themselves to Islamic education. During their time in Pakistan, Afghan Talibs were supported particularly by the *deobandi*, which was in turn financed by Saudi Arabia and the Pakistani ISI. Their particular teaching in *jihad* concentrated on the concept of defence of Muslim land against infidels rather than a struggle against every form of evil. It is clear that the Madrassahs, and by inference the *deobandi* movement, made a significant contribution to the intellectual and practical origins of the Taliban as a fighting force.

Disillusioned with the lack of peace and the moral laxity in Afghanistan, many students discussed what could be done to restore order in their land. The various groups came together early in 1994 around an agenda which remained the public aim of the Taliban when they governed – namely to restore peace, disarm the population, enforce Shariah law and establish a strictly Islamic way of life in Afghanistan.

Mullah Omar emerged as the leader of the movement because of his piety and spirituality. Notoriously secretive and elusive, Mullah Omar explained the intentions of the Taliban in an interview with a Pakistani journalist

> We took up arms to achieve the aims of the Afghan jihad and save our people from further suffering at the hands of the so-called Mujaheddin. We had complete faith in God Almighty. We never forgot that. He can bless us with victory or plunge us into defeat.[3]

Mullah Muhammad Omar has never been photographed and has never met with Western diplomats or journalists. This reluctance to be exposed in the public eye extended even to his movements within Afghanistan itself. He has rarely visited Kabul and while the Taliban were in power in Afghanistan, he stayed in his base in Kandahar, conducting the affairs of state from there.

There are many speculations around the emergence of the Taliban as a credible military and political force. The most reliable story of how this movement came to ascendancy is told repeatedly by Taliban soldiers and we heard a version of it ourselves while in Afghanistan. In 1994 Mullah Omar mobilized a small number of Taliban against the aggressive and abusive warlords of Kandahar. A small group of local people came to him to ask for help – two teenage girls had been kidnapped and taken to the military camp where they were repeatedly raped and had their heads shaved. Omar took 30 students with him and attacked the camp. They rescued the girls and hanged the camp commander, also capturing arms and ammunitions. As word of this story spread Omar found himself being called upon as a kind of Islamic Robin Hood figure. He specialized in freeing ordinary, poor Afghan people from immoral and oppressive warlords.

In mid-1994, Afghan refugees living in the Quetta area of Pakistan, many of whom had been schooled in the Madrassahs, formed themselves into a fighting force and, with some support from Pakistan, crossed the border. These soldiers began by clearing the roads of bandits and marauders so that trucks and convoys could safely travel. This proved to be a lucrative move as the Taliban could charge a fee for the safe travel of goods across the country. By the beginning of 1995 the Taliban had captured Kandahar – the second largest city in Afghanistan.

They immediately implemented a very strict interpretation of Shariah law. Schools were closed to girls, women were forbidden from working outside the home, televisions were outlawed and publicly smashed, sports and recreations were banned and all men were compelled to wear beards of a certain length.

In the following few months the Taliban took control of 12 of the 31 provinces of Afghanistan, opening up the roads for trade and disarming the local population. After the capture of Kandahar over 20,000 Madrassah students streamed over the border from Pakistan to join the forces of Mullah Omar. Many of these were young and inexperienced in war – between the ages of 14 and 25. They had known nothing other than life in a refugee camp or a Madrassah. They knew nothing of their country's pre-war customs and history. They had no economic prospects and no grasp of the complex ethnic and religious mix that made up Afghanistan before and during Soviet occupation. Untrained in any craft or agriculture and often orphaned from their families, this generation of young Pashtu men found a vision and a vocation in fighting for the Taliban. The male brotherhood offered a religious structured life, a cause to die for – a belief that could give meaning and purpose. The early successes in the face of huge improbability gave the movement a momentum and increased the conviction that God was on their side.

Whereas the southern regions governed by chaotic Pashtun commanders had capitulated relatively easily to the Taliban, the movement faced much tougher resistance in the north. President Rabbani had held Kabul in the face of the fighting and siege imposed by an opposition leader Hikmetyar. However, when Hikmetyar's forces found themselves trapped between government forces in the north and Taliban forces in the south they capitulated. The Taliban captured their bases but rather than continuing the tactics of siege they opened up the roads into Kabul. This was an enormously popular move. Despite this move, they were initially unable to capture Kabul which was held by a skilled government commander called General Massoud. The Taliban suffered a great defeat in March 1995 and a few thousand soldiers were killed. Even more died of thirst and basic wounds on the route back to Kandahar.

The image of the Taliban was now badly damaged. Their presentation of themselves as peacemakers and the bringers of Islamic stability was dented by defeat and many Afghans began to see them as just another warring faction.

The Taliban next turned their attention to the west of the country. The beautiful city of Herat which has been the cultural, literary and artistic capital of the nation is predominantly Persian. Herat is situated in the midst of miles of irrigated farmland which is rimmed by mountains. Herodotus described Herat as the "breadbasket of Central Asia" and for centuries the city was the crossroads of the Turkic and Persian empires. Beautiful mosques, baths, libraries and palaces were built here and Herat came to be associated with fine Persian poetry and painting.

Herat prided itself on its sophisticated education system, educating both girls and boys even in the difficult circumstances of Soviet occupation and the ensuing civil war. In September of 1995 the Taliban took Herat without firing a single shot. The Taliban forces proved too much of a threat to the beleaguered government forces. When the Taliban had taken Kandahar they had closed all but three of the 45 schools. Now in Herat, the seat of learning for the nation, they closed all of the schools and outlawed girls even studying at home. Shariah law and the banning of all entertainment were implemented fiercely. The cultured Persian population was now occupied by a group of uneducated Pashtuns.

The capture of Herat gave the Taliban control of the west of the country and the trade routes through Turkmenistan and into Europe. Bolstered by their success they went on to capture Kabul in September 1996 after a lengthy siege. Televisions, videos, satellite dishes, all music, and all games including chess and kite flying were banned. Men without beards were arrested and all women were banned from working even though some 25% of Kabul's civil service and a large proportion of the education system and health service were staffed by women. Radio Kabul was renamed Radio Shariat and announced that thieves would have hands and feet amputated and adulterers would be stoned.[4]

The Taliban by now controlled most of Afghanistan's population; however, the remaining stronghold Mazar-E-Sharif remained under the control of General Dostum along with around 60% of Afghanistan's agriculture and 80% of its former industry and mineral resources. The Taliban were determined to unite the whole country and they set their sights toward the north. This proved to be the most difficult of the Afghan territories to capture. Under the guidance of General Dostum the Taliban suffered a bloody defeat which was compounded by the subsequent re-emergence of fighting in Kabul. An anti-Taliban alliance, however, fell apart and in August 1998 and with the help of thousands more troops marshalled in Pakistan, the Taliban took Mazar. Their entrance into the city was bloody and brutal as the soldiers vented their frustration at their previous losses.

Ethnic Persecution

Now that the Taliban had begun to take areas of Afghanistan in which Pashtus were not the dominant racial group, ethnic tensions emerged. Shi'ite Muslims from the Hazara ethnic group were massacred in a village south of Mazar and Tajik farmers were forced out of the Shomali valley.[5] When the Taliban took Mazar they went on a killing spree murdering men, women and children. The bodies of the dead lay unburied in the streets for days. Indiscriminate killing went hand in hand with particular targeting of the Hazara people. Thousands of Hazaras were taken to the jail and put into containers where they were left to suffocate and die.[6]

The Taliban now aimed to rid the north of Afghanistan of Shi'ite Islam entirely. From the central mosque in Mazar this message was preached: "The Hazaras are not Muslims …You either accept to be Muslims or you leave Afghanistan. Wherever you go we will catch you."[7] The UN estimated that between 5,000 and 6,000 Uzbeks and Tajiks were massacred along the Taliban's route to Mazar. The combination of religious extremism and racial prejudice was fatal.

Politics and Economics

The Taliban's arrival in Afghanistan was swift and in the course of one year they took over half the country, suppressing gangs of robbers and factions. The advance from Quetta has been on the strategic road through Afghanistan which goes on to Central Asia and Russia. This trade route is a valuable link with the world and it seems that Pakistan encouraged the Taliban to take it, as the Taliban were able to eradicate the many factions along the road. Ahmed Shah Massoud, who controlled President Rabbani's government, accused the Taliban of being created by the Pakistani Secret Service and by its Interior Minister General Nasseerullah Khan Barbar. He called the Taliban leaders: "puppets of Pakistan even if their foot soldiers are unaware of the links."[8] A former member of Pakistan's Senate called Hafiz Hussain Ahmed attempted to explain the origins of the Taliban:

The Taliban movement is a new movement in Afghanistan, but it is also the continuation of the Holy War. For America and Europe that war finished when the Soviet Union pulled out. But for the younger generation of Afghanistan it still hasn't achieved its purpose. And when they saw that their sacrifice was fruitless, it was natural that this movement would come to the boil and that they would return.[9]

Alongside the involvement of Pakistan through the Madrassahs, the question of other foreign influence as a factor in the emergence of the Taliban movement cannot be ignored. It seems that the countries surrounding Afghanistan encouraged the war as it made the country weak and preoccupied. General Massoud voiced this by explaining that he wanted Afghanistan to be independent of surrounding countries but as the Taliban have such close links with Pakistan he had to accept help from Pakistan's rivals India, Iran and Russia.

Before the escalation of events in September 2001, the decrease in world interest in Afghanistan after the Soviet Union pulled out was also a factor in creating the context from within which the Taliban movement could spring up. While he was still in power in Kabul in May 1996, President Rabbani lamented the lack of outside interest:

If the world is interested in Human Rights why after 14 years of war have they forgotten Afghanistan? No one cares about the harshness of life for people here – no one cares about ending foreign interference in Afghan affairs; if they had, and foreign interference had stopped and then reconstruction work started, the war would have stopped and the people could get on with life, going to school or university instead of the front line.[10]

The foreign influence Rabbani refers to here is the millions of Cold War dollars pumped into funding the Mujahedin during Russian occupation. This is because in the absence of any Russians to fight, the money and weapons were used against his government by the Mujahedin and some had even fallen into the hands of the Taliban.

Rabbani also objected to the foreign financial support given to the Taliban. The arrival of the Taliban in Kandahar featured a fleet of new Land Rovers and sophisticated communications technology. Two years on in Herat, Taliban government departments were equipped with satellite telephone networks while the rest of the city struggled without electricity. The Taliban's logistics and communications were inexplicably sophisticated for a largely illiterate guerrilla movement.

Oil

In November 1995 the headquarters of a joint venture by Saudi Arabian and United States oil companies opened in Islamabad. The venture is the construction of an oil pipeline stretching from the Caspian Sea, north of Afghanistan, through what was Taliban territory and then on to Pakistan and the Indian ocean. The pipeline, which bypasses Iran, would lessen worldwide dependence on the Middle East for oil.[11] It seems that United States companies, Saudi Arabia and Pakistan all contributed financially to the Taliban movement.

The Terrorist Haven

During the war against the Soviets, Muslims were recruited from around the world to fight with the Mujahedin in Afghanistan. The Inter Services Intelligence in Pakistan set up reception committees in order to welcome the new recruits and direct them to training centres from where they could join the Mujahedin. A good deal of the funding for the training of these Islamic militants came from Saudi Arabia. Oliver Roy called this "a joint venture between the Saudis, the Muslim brotherhood and the Jamaat-e-Islami put together by the ISI."[12] What began as Islamic camps for training volunteers to help defeat the Soviets in Afghanistan became a network of extremist centres intent on bringing "pure" Islam to the world by means of *jihad*. Between 1982 and 1992 around 35,000 Muslims militants from 43 different countries would pass through this military training. When the Soviets were defeated in Afghanistan, this was seen as a divine victory for

Islam against all the odds. A superpower defeated by a holy army with inferior firepower and expertise.

In the wake of this inspiring military victory in Afghanistan, the international networks of extremists remained. Samuel Huntingdon commented that:

> The war ... left a legacy of expert and experienced fighters, training camps and logistical facilities, elaborate trans-Islam networks of personal and organization relationships, a substantial amount of military equipment including 300 to 500 unaccounted for Stinger missiles, and, most important, a heady sense of power and self-confidence over what had been achieved and a driving desire to move on to other victories.[13]

Osama bin Laden and Al Qaeda

Among the many thousands of recruits was a Saudi-born graduate called Osama Bin Laden. His wealthy father had helped to fund the Afghan struggle and was supportive of his son going to participate. Bin Laden gave generously to the cause and in 1989 set up Al Qaeda (al-Qa'ida), a network which was to be a support service to non-Afghan Muslims who had come to join the fight against the Soviets.

After returning to Saudi Arabia in the 1990s Bin Laden offered his network of trained militants to push the Iraqis out of Kuwait. He was extremely disappointed when the Saudi Kingdom instead allied with the USA and allowed American militia to be based in the Islamic Holy Kingdom. After spending some time in Sudan, Bin Laden moved to Afghanistan in 1996 and in 1997 struck up a friendship with Mullah Omar. Afghanistan became his base and he began to grow in influence with the Taliban. Having significantly contributed funds and personnel to the Taliban's Holy War effort Bin Laden's anti-Western ethos began to be reflected in the Taliban's outlook.

The habouring of Islamic radical terrorists and the close relationship with Osama bin Laden in particular, proved to be fatal for the Taliban. That which had begun as a reforming religious movement, aiming to end fighting and corruption in Afghanistan, emerged as a radical and oppressive regime. The international prominence and notoriety of the Taliban further increased as radical terrorists, trained on Afghan soil and protected by the Taliban, threatened violence and destruction around the world.

The Drug Trade

Tony Buckingham, Director of the United Nations Drug Control Program in South West Asia, said that: "Afghanistan is one of the biggest producers of opiates in the world. It accounts for seventy percent of the heroin supplied to Western Europe."[14] When the Taliban stormed across Afghanistan in 1994 bringing with them the puritanical form of Islam that has become their hallmark, they promised to root out the opium poppy once and for all. The use of drugs is prohibited by Islam and the following extract from a well-known thirteenth-century CE Muslim scholar Shaikh al-Islam ibn Taymiyyah, elucidates the general Muslim attitude toward drugs:

> This solid grass is prohibited, whether or not it produces intoxication. Sinful people smoke it because they find it produces rapture and delight, an effect similar to drunkenness. While wine makes the one who drinks it active and quarrelsome, hashish produces dullness and lethargy; furthermore, smoking it disturbs the mind and temperament, excites sexual desire, and leads to shameless promiscuity, and these are greater evils than those caused by drinking.[15]

Despite this, production of opium in 1996 in Afghanistan was far higher even than it was in 1995 – especially in Taliban controlled areas. When questioned about this the Taliban Minister of Health Mullah Ibrahim Baluch answered saying:

> The Taliban are very much against drugs because they are forbidden under Islamic Law. But our people are very poor and only

have a small amount of land and if they are to grow wheat or another crop, they do not get as much profit as they would from growing poppies. So poverty is the main culprit. At the moment we are too busy with our struggle to tackle the problem.[16]

As the Taliban clearly had the time to enforce other strict measures such as forbidding television and music and keeping women out of the workplace, this is somewhat dubious.

One anonymous observer in Herat who feared for his life explained that: "drug traffickers have successfully infiltrated the Taliban. The international Mafia and those who traffic drugs outside Afghanistan are supporters of the Taliban Movement."[17] It has in fact emerged that although in the past the equipment for processing and transporting opium was always based outside Afghanistan itself, under Taliban jurisdiction the necessary machinery and equipment was brought in to the country. This is probably because the return is higher on more refined substances. The opium goes through Iran and the heroin through Turkmenistan and because the Taliban cleared the crucial roads of bandits and mines the whole transportation process has been made easier.

When the Taliban first came to power they insisted that there would be no half-hearted observance of the Qur'an yet the expenses incurred by war seemed to persuade them to overlook the sins of producing, refining and trafficking drugs. Another justification came in the light of the fact that the drugs are exported: "Opium is permissible because it is consumed by kafirs (unbelievers) in the West and not by Muslims and Afghans" but hashish is banned by the Taliban because "it is consumed by Afghans and Muslims."[18] The money from the drug trade went into the coffers of the Taliban and the terrorist networks they hosted. The money was used to finance the expensive Holy War within Afghanistan itself and beyond. This anomaly of radical, puritanical Islamic groups pursuing a holy war in the world funded in part by the sale of forbidden substances highlights the contradictions surrounding the Taliban and Al Qaeda.

For decades Afghanistan has been a country which produces a large proportion of the world's illegal substances and both the Mujahedin and the former government of President Rabbani used revenue from the drugs trade to fund war. In this moral question the Taliban did not prove themselves to be a new force in Afghanistan as they were not able to put the requirements of "pure Islam" before their political and ideological struggle. Indeed, the Taliban quickly formalized the drug economy in order to raise revenue, collecting 20% of the value of a truckload of opium as a tax. It has conservatively been estimated that around one million Afghan farmers are making over US$100 million a year through growing poppies. The Taliban were then receiving at least US$20 million a year from this enterprise.

The Taliban movement's origins are not only strongly rooted in religious fervour, cultivated in the Madrassahs of Pakistan, but also in the political and economic context of the region – this includes not only the rivalries of Afghanistan's neighbours Pakistan, India, Iran and Russia – but also the historic Cold War animosity between the Soviet Union and the United States along with the economic rivalry over oil between Middle East countries and with the United States.

---

[1] Pashtuns make up some 40 percent of Afghanistan's 20 million people.

[2] *The Independent*, 18 February 1997.

[3] Yousufzai, *News*, 2 February 1995.

[4] The Pakastani Ambassador to Italy commented at a private dinner on 16 October 2001 that the Taliban had brought about a fantastic drop in the crime statistics. "If somebody steals something their hand is cut off. This has been very effective – it is now safe to walk the streets in Afghanistan."

[5] Peters, Gretchen, "Massacres prompt fears of ethnic escalation", AP, 15 February 1997.

[6] ibid.

[7] Yousufzai, "Dostum unearths mass graves", *News*, 16 November 1997.

[8] British Film Institute: Interview by John Simpson, Head of BBC Foreign News. *Newsnight*, 2 May 1996.

[9] *Newsnight*, 2 May 1996.

[10] *Newsnight*, 1 May 1996.

[11] Anthony Hyman: Central Asian Survey. Lecture at Oxford Centre for Islamic Studies, 12 February 1997.

[12] Roy, *Afghanistan, From Holy War to Civil War,* p. 29.

[13] Huntingdon, *The Clash of Civilisations.*

[14] *Newsnight*, 3 May 1996.

[15] Ibn Taymiyyay, *Fatawa,* vol. 4, p. 262.

[16] *Newsnight*, 3 May 1996.

[17] Interview F.I.l. Orr-Ewing, M. Toulmin, A. Kopsch, April 1996.

[18] Interview with Abdul Rashid Kandahar cited in Rashid, *Taliban, Islam Oil,* p. 118.

4

Women and Islam

The poor treatment of women in some Islamic countries is an issue that is widely discussed in the West. This facet of Islam, most particularly practiced by extreme Islamic movements, has caught the attention of the media on many occasions. Afghanistan's Taliban were known in the world for their emphasis on women's issues. Indeed, the outlawing of education and vocation for women was a well-publicized development. However, although an extreme example, the Taliban do not stand alone as an Islamic regime which has oppressed women. In this chapter we will attempt to discover if there is any precedent or justification for repressive attitudes toward women in the texts and traditions of Islam.

Historical Development

How does the traditional role of women in Islam relate to their treatment at the hands of the Taliban and other Islamist regimes? Recent studies suggest that the salient features associated with the treatment of women in Islamic society had already developed in the East by the seventh century when Islam first began.[1] Subordination of women "resulted from the gradual evolution of the social and economic conditions that existed in the Middle East since Neolithic times".[2] Because agriculture assumed an increasingly larger share as a source of revenue in the region, so a greater division of labour within the community was effected. Men began to play a larger role in the field while women devoted most of their time to child-bearing and domestic activities. The rise of urban life which appeared first in Mesopotamia accelerated this existing division of labour between men and women, further reduced women's economic power and fostered a development of attitudes which held them to an inferior position in society.

Within a few decades of Muhammad's death in 632, the Arabian Muslims had conquered much of the Middle East. As an increasing number of people from the defeated areas embraced Islam, the status of women was progressively undermined. The culture of the conquered population, who vastly outnumbered the early Muslims of Arabian origin, was taken on and assimilated into the religion. Women were increasingly viewed as inferior to men; descent through the father was emphasized; effort was made to minimize contact between male strangers and women; and women's tasks were confined to household duties.

Some of the theologians who were developing and interpreting religious law at this time were themselves of non-Arab stock.[3] In their debates over the proper mode of behaviour for Muslim women, they argued in such a way as to interpret Qur'anic references to women in a manner reflecting their own cultural values. This may explain why in many cases the Qur'anic statements regarding women are less restrictive than the eventual provisions that appear in the Shariah. In the first century after the Qur'an was received Muslim ideology concerning the role of women became increasingly restrictive, influenced by cultural maxims.

Contemporary Era

Some Islamic regimes in the contemporary period demonstrate treatment of women that is both harsh and restrictive. Strict segregation of the sexes is an integral part of Saudi Arabian society, for example, and has adverse and unequal effects on women. Women are denied equal educational opportunities and may work only in certain vocations. The freedom of movement is severely restricted for women and they may only travel abroad if they have the written authorization of a male relative. They may even have to be accompanied. Inside Saudi Arabia, women are forbidden to drive, a ban made official in 1990 by a fatwa issued by the Council of Senior 'Ulama (influential religious scholars) who interpret the law.

Some laws in Saudi Arabia are discriminatory in their application rather than articulation. The offence of khilwa (being alone with a male who is not an immediate relative) is punishable for both men and women, but it seems to be more frequently enforced against women. To walk unaccompanied or to be in the company of a man who is neither her husband nor a close relative puts a woman at risk of arrest on suspicion of prostitution or other similar offences. Women, whether Saudi Arabian or foreign, frequently become victims of discrimination because of the law, social mores and traditions of the country.[4]

While women in Saudi Arabia have progressed in terms of economic rights and have been able to set up companies and charitable institutions, their civil, political and social rights are systematically undermined. An American official visiting Riyadh in 2001 commented on the press reports from Afghanistan about the oppression of women and religious minorities. He observed:

> Virtually everything described there was taking place in Saudi Arabia, with the exception that at least the Taliban permitted other religions to exist in their country. This is absolutely forbidden in Saudi Arabia.[5]

Saudi Arabia and Afghanistan are not alone among Islamic states in restrictive legislation against women. In 1978–9 clerical revolutionaries in Iran unleashed a series of forces which transformed and reshaped the face of Iranian society. These clerics placed themselves above any worldly legislature and claimed authority from God to interpret and establish his laws on earth. The changes which were implemented have negatively affected women's social, political and economic status in Iran.[6]

Before the Revolution, Iran was ruled by Reza Shah Pahlavi who introduced a period of economic revitalization. One of his major accomplishments was the improvement of the status of women within the country. The Shah's reforms included making the wearing of the *chador* or veil against the law, opening up the educational system to women at the primary, secondary, and post-secondary levels, and allowing women access to employment opportunities.[7] In the mid-1940s Reza Shah Pahlavi resigned in favour of his son Mohamad Reza Shah. The new Shah was also committed to the social renewal of the country and he followed in his father's footsteps attempting to modernize. He famously passed the Family Protection Act of 1975 which increased the rights of women significantly.[8] The Act also reduced the influence of Islamic law on society and in particular on women. The Family Protection Act gave women increased civil rights in marriage, child custody, and divorce. Men were prevented from unilateral divorce, and in cases of child custody, the family court was given the power to decide which parent would assume custody.[9]

The Islamic Revolution of 1978–9 brought a dramatic reversal to the tendency toward secularizing the country. Islam became the official new state ideology and the clerical elites gained political power. Iran's *Islamic* Constitution explains that: "the basic characteristic of the Islamic Revolution, which distinguishes it from other movements that have taken place in Iran during the past hundred years, is its ideological and Islamic nature."[10] Such a clear emphasis on Islam as the centre of governance had profound implications for Iranian society. The 1979 Islamic Constitution resulted in a shift of the legal system from a secular to religious orientation.

In the Islamic Republic of Iran the ultimate source of law became the will of Allah as made known in the Qur'an. However, issues of interpretation naturally arose because of differences among jurists, whether Sunni or Shi'ite Muslims or conservative or moderate. The case of *Soraya M* gives us an illustration of the implications of these developments for some

women in Iran.[11] From 1979 to 1994 more than one thous-
and women have been stoned to death in Iran.

The senior Iranian cleric Khomeini had certain perceptions
and views of the position of women in a society governed by
Islamic law. Khomeini, in interpreting the Islamic laws,
wrote:

> A woman who has been contracted permanently must not leave
> the house without the husband's permission and must surrender
> herself for any pleasure that he wants and must not prevent him
> from having intercourse with her without religious excuse. If she
> ... obeys the husband must [provide] her [with] food and clothing
> and dwelling, and other appliances and if he does not provide
> them then he is indebted to the woman.[12]

This line of thinking was developed at the Islamic Council of
Guardians in Iran:

> a woman does not have the right to leave her home without her
> husband's permission, not even to attend her father's funeral ... A
> woman is completely at service of her husband, and her social
> activities are conditional upon her husband's permission.[13]

The tenets of the 1975 Family Protection Act were rejected by
the Islamic regime in Iran. In today's Iran, men can obtain a
unilateral divorce from their wife or wives. The marriage age
for females has been lowered to nine and in some instances to
seven.[14] Mothers no longer have equal rights in terms of child
custody.

At the outset of the revolution when Khomeini re-imposed
the veil and other strict Islamic mandates, thousands of
women took to the streets demanding back their rights. The
show of force and the number of protesters forced the regime
to ease its demand. It was only later, once the regime was
established, that these laws were once again introduced and
made part of the legal system. These include the mandatory
wearing of the veil, prohibition on inter-gender contact and
restrictions on political activity.

The situation for women in Iran, Afghanistan and Saudi Arabia demonstrates the reality of Islamist interpretations of the Qur'an and traditions. These same texts and source materials have been used by moderates in more progressive Muslim states to try and integrate women into professions and give women an equal status in society, for example, in Turkey. And yet the Islamist justification for their repression of women is rooted in Islamic scripture and tradition.

The Texts and Traditions

It is interesting that in Islamic countries from across the spectrum, whether traditionalist or progressive, the authority for ideology, law and practice is drawn from the Qur'an and the Shariah. Interpretation of these source materials is claimed as the authenticating authority for all sides of the debate. For any kind of appraisal of the issues involved, the most constructive method is probably to look at the words of the Qur'an and the *Hadith* themselves. The earliest messages of the Qur'an and the twin themes which run throughout all the chapters are of the realities of the *Tauhid*, or the oneness of God, and the inevitability of the Day of Judgement. All persons, whether men or women, are called upon to testify to these realities. But there is a tradition that Umm Salama, one of Muhammad's wives, reminded him that he was saying "men" only when he meant both men and women.[15] After this reminder we are told that he clearly identified both believing men and believing women as fully responsible for their religious duties and fully accountable at the time of the final judgement. In Sura 33:35 this is made clear:

> The self-surrendering men and the self-surrendering women, the believing men and the believing women, the obedient men and the obedient women, the truthful men and the truthful women, the enduring men and the enduring women, the submissive men and the submissive women, the almsgiving men and the almsgiving women, the continent men and the continent women, the

Allah-remembering men and the Allah-remembering women – for
them Allah has prepared forgiveness and a mighty reward.

The religious duties imposed by Islam on the faithful apply to
women just as much as to men.[16]

However, in the Qur'an there do appear to be some statements that imply the inferiority of women. Sura 4:11 states that
women can inherit only half of what men can inherit: "God
charges you, concerning your children: to the male the like of
the portion of two females." Some Muslims have argued that
this is not as discriminatory as it sounds because the woman's
inheritance is entirely for her own use, while the man must
keep no private resources for himself but should use all financial assets at his disposal to supply for the family. However,
the fact that the witness in a court of law of one man is equal
to that of two women seems to confirm the lower status of
women in society: "And call into witness two witnesses, men,
or if the two be not men, then one man and two women, such
witnesses as you approve of, that if one of the two errs the
other will remind her" (Sura 2:282).

There are many stories in the *Hadith* which are
unfavourable to the status of women. One such example suggests that the majority of women will be in the fire on the Day
of Judgement because of their mental and physical inferiority.
Muhammad is reported to have said: "I stood at the gates of
Paradise, most of those who entered there were poor, I stood
at the gates of Hell, most of those who went in there were
women."[17] Muhammad is alleged to have said: "If it is proper
for a human being to kneel in adoration to another human
being, then this is only for a woman to kneel to a man."[18]
Another statement Muhammad made about women which
casts a shadow over female leadership is found in the *Hadith*:
"A people which entrusts its affairs to a woman will have no
success."[19]

In the Qur'an, women are only allowed to instigate divorce
proceedings for a set number of reasons whereas a man needs
no specific pretext at all. Because the male rules the whole
house, the religion of the male is taken to be the religion of the

household thus, although Muslim men are free to marry a Jewish or a Christian woman, a Muslim female may only marry another Muslim (Sura 5:6). It is permissible in Islam for a man to marry up to four wives; however, a woman may marry only one husband. These practical stipulations for the order of society may underlie some of the poor treatment of women that has developed in the Islamic world.

One scholar comments that within Islam "discipline (Sura 4:34) and sex (Sura 2:223) are the prerogatives of the male to which the female is subject."[20] The Qur'an and the *Hadith* have much to say about the role of women in Islam and it is possible to see how, over the centuries, efforts at interpreting this material by Muslims have led to a belief in the essential inferiority of women in some quarters. In the context of divorce the Qur'an says: "... they (women) have the same right as is exercised over them, though the men have a rank above them" (Sura 2: 228). The inferiority of women is even clearer in other verses, for example:

> The men are overseers over the women by reason of what Allah hath bestowed in bounty upon one more than another, and of the property which they have contributed. Upright women are therefore submissive, guarding what is hidden in return for Allah's guarding [them]; those on whose part you fear refractoriness, admonish, avoid in bed, and beat, if they then obey you, seek no [further] way against them (Sura 4:34,38).

If the particular passages in the *Hadith* that reflect attitudes towards women are examined closely, it soon becomes apparent that they contain a wide range of views some of which appear to be in tension. For example, in one place Muhammad is reported as having said: "The whole world is delightful, but the most delightful thing in it is a virtuous woman"[21] and yet in another the following is also attributed to him: "I have left behind no temptation more harmful to my community than that which women represent for men."[22] This somewhat muddled view of women and their role is reflected in the spectrum of treatment within the Islamic world over the centuries, ranging from respect and admiration to suppression and humiliation.

Muslim Feminism

It may be hard for outsiders to understand how repressive approaches to women can still abound and be acceptable to women from within the tradition itself. One writer comments that:

> It is difficult for Western feminists to grasp exactly what the Muslim woman may mean by liberation. For many Islamic women, the fruits of liberation in the West are too many broken marriages, women left without the security of men who will provide for them and deteriorating relations between men and women.[23]

The argument follows the line that Muslim women perceive the Islamic system as defined by the Qur'an as one in which male authority over them ensures their care and protection and provides a structure in which the family is solid. It is even asserted that many Muslim women welcome being dominated by men and see their role as supporter of their husband and that Westerners must accept "a point of view that is more and more prevalent."[24] This, however, is not the whole story as can be seen when the views of other Muslim feminists are appraised.

The Role of Arabic Culture

The publicist Qasim Amin published a book in 1899 entitled *The Liberation of Women,* in which he commented that the oppression of women in Islamic countries did not have its origin in Islam but in the culture into which Islam was revealed. This culture had been absorbed into the religion. He cites examples of Muhammad's wives accompanying him on various expeditions and tending the sick.

Other feminist readings of the Qur'an and *Hadith* portray Muhammad's wives as dynamic, influential and enterprising members of the community who participated fully in Muslim public affairs. The women were "not just background figures, but shared with him his strategic concerns. He listened to their advice, which was sometimes the deciding factor in thorny negotiations."[25] Some feminists have argued that it was certain male members of the community who were not ready to accept such female power, and organized opposition under the leadership of Umar ibn al-Khattab. Muhammad was then forced to sacrifice his egalitarian vision for the sake of unity and the survival of the Islamic cause.[26] Thus to Islamic feminists the seclusion of Muhammad's wives from public life, exemplified in the adoption of the veil or *hijab* in Sura 33:53, is a symbol of Islam's retreat from an early principle of gender equality.

The Veil

Much has been said and written about the wearing of the veil by women in Islam and although there is no binding obligation for it in the Qur'an there are suggestions as in the 33rd Sura: "O prophet say to thy wives, and thy daughters, and the women-folk of the believers, that they let down some of their mantles over them; that is more suitable for their being recognized and not insulted" (Sura 33:59). Another verse which is often quoted as evidence of an exhortation to women to veil themselves is:

> Tell the believing women to cast down their eyes and guard their private parts and not show their ornaments, except so far as they appear, and let them throw their scarves over their bosoms and not show their ornaments except to their husbands or their fathers or the fathers of their husbands, or their sons or the sons of their husbands, or their brothers or the sons of their brothers, or the sons of their sisters, or their womenfolk, or those in their possession (Sura 24:31).

In neither of these passages is the veiling of the face specific-ally mentioned; in fact, the second verse seems to assume that certain parts of the body were visible anyway. Opponents of veiling such as Jahiz[27] in the ninth century have also pointed out that while on a pilgrimage, one of the "pillars" of Islam, men and women are required to have their faces and hands uncovered to be in the ritual state of *ihram* (ritual consecration).

Even before the advent of Islam the noble ladies of the trading city of Mecca wore veils. In fact, the veil already existed in the countries of the ancient Near East captured by the Muslims. Among the Assyrians and the Babylonians, the veil was a symbol of class distinction. It was the right of free women to wear it. In contrast any slave who wore it was liable to be punished. Thus an early Arabian historian explains Sura 33:59 in this way – Muhammad's wives had been bothered by his opponents in Medina when they left the house at night to relieve themselves, because they took unveiled women for slaves and Muhammad wrote the verses then to protect his wives from misunderstanding in the culture in which they lived.[28] Whatever Muhammad's intentions in writing these verses about the veil, the fact remains that they have been used by many Muslims to strongly encourage and at times enforce the wearing of the veil for women.

Veils traditionally have taken a number of forms; a veil which covers the face from just below the eyes down; a *chador* or *burke* which cover the entire body including the face with a woven grill through which women can see but not be seen; and a full face mask with small slits for the eyes. These veils are like a symbol of oppression for many Westerners and indeed a general movement for unveiling within Islam had an ostensible beginning in the mid-1920s when the Egyptian feminist Huda Sha'rawi cast off her veil after arriving in Egypt from an international meeting of women. She was followed literally and symbolically by many women in the succeeding years.

Current trends

At the present time, however, quite a different phenomenon is found within Islam. This takes the form of a reaction against what are seen as Western liberal moral standards, in which Muslim women are consciously adopting forms of dress by which they can identify with Islam rather than with the West. Rana Kabbani writes on this subject that:

> Wearing the hijab can be a liberation, freeing women from being sexual objects, releasing them from the trap of Western dress and the dictates of Western fashion. Just as feminists in the West have reflected on the connection between "feminine" clothes and female oppression, so Muslim feminists reject the outward symbols of sexual allure. In favour of the hijab it can be said that by distancing its wearer from the world it enriches spiritual life, grants freedom from material preoccupations, and erases class differences by expressing solidarity with others in the same uniform. Since all women look the same in it, it is a most effective equalizer, and since it camouflages rich clothing, it is in keeping with the Islamic injunction against ostentation.[29]

This suggests that there is a growing strain of feminism in Islam which sees itself as voluntarily adopting traditional Muslim customs and dress in defiance of slipping Western moral standards. Unfortunately, not all Muslim women, least of all those under regimes like Afghanistan's Taliban, have had such a choice and it is perhaps the *enforcing* of such a dramatic form of traditional dress that has caused resentment and disagreement.

The Taliban and Women

The plight of Afghan women began before the arrival of the Taliban. Over twenty years of unremitting war had destroyed the very infrastructure of society. The traditional expressions of family life and tribal community had been eroded by the harsh reality of bloodshed and fighting. A staggeringly high number of Afghan women die in childbirth[30] and the infant mortality rate is also far beyond that of other developing countries.[31] Illiteracy was a huge problem before the Taliban came to power affecting 90% of girls and 60% of boys. The Taliban's policies on gender only served to make the difference worse.

The Taliban insisted that women wear the *burka* – which covers the entire body including the face. On taking Kabul in 1996 the Taliban issued many decrees which were to be enforced by the religious police. For example:

> Women you should not step outside your residence. If you go outside the house you should not be like women who used to go with fashionable clothes wearing much cosmetics and appearing in front of every man before the coming of Islam. Islam as a rescuing religion has determined specific dignity for women, Islam has valuable instructions for women … If women are going outside with fashionable, ornamental, tight and charming clothes to show themselves, they will be cursed by the Islamic Shari'a and should never expect to go to heaven.[32]

The Taliban even stipulated the kind of cover women should wear: the Pashtu *burka*:

> To prevent sedition and female uncovers. No drivers are allowed to pick up women who are using Iranian burqa. In case of violation the driver will be imprisoned. If such kind of female are observed in the street their house will be found and their husband punished. If the women use stimulating and attractive cloth and there is no accompany of close male relative with them, the drivers should not pick them up.[33]

This is an extreme interpretation of the Qur'anic advice on modesty and propriety and it has been argued by many that the Taliban were merely enforcing their own preferred cultural maxims on women rather than Islamic law. While it is possible to see from some passages of the Qur'an and *Hadith* that the veiling of women should lead to female piety and morality, the edicts of the Taliban were heavily influenced by their own Pashtu cultural background.

The same is not true for the involvement of women in the world of work – nowhere in the Qur'an is the education or employment of women prohibited. Even other Islamist regimes have allowed women to work in various if limited fields of employment. But upon conquering an area of Afghanistan the Taliban consistently banned women from working at all: "Women have the responsibility as a teacher or coordinator for her family. Husband, brother, father have the responsibility for providing the family with necessary life requirements (food, clothes etc)."[34] However, when pressed as to the reasoning behind preventing women from working, the Taliban answer is practical rather than theological. The comments which recur time and time again when pressed on this issue was that they feared for the safety of women and wanted to protect them.[35] The Taliban are horrified at pictures of women in the West: "They look so tired – we do not want our women to be tired." They also believe that home is the safest place for women to be: "In our country it is not safe for women to be outside for long."[36]

It seems that the Taliban's extraordinary attitude toward women was dictated by their interpretation of passages in the Qur'an and *Hadith*, their perception of Islamic purity, and genuine concerns for the safety of women in war-torn Afghanistan.

Prior to the arrival of the Taliban in Afghanistan, women had been at great risk from marauding groups of soldiers from many different factions who regularly raped and killed young girls and older women. One of the comments of a local farmer from Kandahar expressed the relief felt when the Taliban came bringing such a strict regime: "I am sorry about the literacy of my girls, but grateful for the security that these Talibs have brought to our region. I no longer fear for their safety." The kind of Islam that the Taliban were presenting Afghanistan with was not new in the sense of having no roots or precedent in Islamic history – indeed the cultural and the religious have rarely been distinguished in the practice of Islam over the centuries.

The Taliban attempted to apply the traditions of Islam strictly, which has through the ages been "a straight path" encompassing every area of life. The overlap of social, political, religious and cultural expressions has been a reality within Islam since the days of Muhammad. The final prophet of Islam was in his own day both a political and a religious figure, a judge of civil and social disputes, a charismatic figure who influenced the religious practices as well as the social customs of his fellow men and women.

The plight of women in many Muslim countries around the world is well known. The Taliban in Afghanistan were a vivid example of a problem which has found expression in various parts of the Islamic world. Islamists and supporters of extreme Islamic regimes cite the Qur'an and traditions of the faith to support legislation and practice which discriminates against women. Many Muslims would not agree with these interpretations, but the fact remains that the repression of women is justified and practiced by those who seek to return to a "pure Islam" based on the Scriptures and history of the faith.

---

[1]   See Walther, *Women in Islam*.

[2]   Ibid. See Introduction by Guity Nashat, p. 5.

[3]   Watt, *Muhammad at Medina*.

[4]   For more information on the position of women in Saudi Arabia see Amnesty International website www.amnestyinternational.org

[5]   Washington post: http://www.washingtonpost.com/wp-dyn/articles/A15193-2001Dec21.html

[6]   Eshghipour, *The Islamic Revolution's Impact*.

[7]   Shawcross, *The Shah's Last Ride*, p. 53.

[8]   Zolan, *The Effects of Islamization*, p. 191.

[9]   This was different from the traditional practice of giving the child to the father or the nearest male relative. Zolan, p.191

[10]   Hunter, *Iran After Khomeini*, p. 1.

[11]   Sahebjam, *The Stoning of Soraya M.*, p. 81. Soraya M. was accused of adultery by her husband Gorban-Ali. Gorban-Ali wanted to get out of his marriage, and was aided by the village authorities, as well as the nature of Islamic law, to successfully accuse and condemn his wife of having sexual relations outside the marriage. Consequently, Soraya was convicted and later was stoned to death for a crime which she had not committed. Under Islamic law, the husband needs to produce two male eyewitnesses in order to win a case of matrimonial infidelity. The

accused woman has the impossible task of proving her innocence. As in the case of *Soraya M.*, the whole town turned against her simply on the basis of unproved accusations. From the mayor of the village to Soraya's family members, her guilt was predetermined and had already been decided. Here the clerical judges were not accountable to review by a higher court.

[12] Zolan, p. 188.

[13] Goodwin, *Price of Honor*, p. 113.

[14] Ibid.

[15] *Husn al-uswa*, Sadiq Hasan Khan, p. 117.

[16] An exception to this can be found in the restrictions placed on menstruating women who are freed from prayer and from certain rituals of pilgrimage and fasting. Despite the fact that these restrictions which are tied up with the religious uncleanness of menstruating women, are few in number; from them a body of arguments have been built up establishing the inferiority of women in the religious sphere.

[17] *Musnad*, vol. 1, 137 by Ahmad Ibn Hanbal.

[18] 120, VI, 411.

[19] 24, 92, 18

[20] Rippin, *Muslims: Their Religious Beliefs and Practices*, Vol 2, p. 119.

[21] 82, II, 168.

[22] 82, V, 200.

[23] Sharma, A. (ed.), *Women in World Religions*, p. 249.

[24] Ibid.

[25] Mernissi, *The Veil and the Male Elite*, p. 104.

[26] Stowasser, *Women in the Qu'ran, Tradition and Interpretation*, p. 133.

[27] Walther, *Women in Islam*, p. 70.

[28] 87, VIII, 126ff.

[29] Kabbani, *Letter to Christendom*, p. 27.

[30] 1700 mothers out of 100,000 giving birth die.

[31] 163 out of 1,000 births.

[32] Cited in Rashid *Taliban Islam, Oil*, p. 217.

[33] Ibid, p.218

[34] Ibid, p.217.

[35] Our own interview 1996.

[36] Interview by Caroline Lees in *The Spectator*, November 1996.

5

The Clash of Civilizations

In *The West's Encounter with Islam*, Monshipouri states:

> Relations between the Muslim and Western worlds have replaced
> the Soviet-Western standoff on the centre stage in the post-Cold
> War era. Although political and economic issues have garnered
> greater attention than religious issues in the current global context,
> it has become fashionable to speculate about the cultural conflicts
> between Muslim and Western worlds. Some Western observers
> have concentrated attention on Islamic radicalism and militancy,
> depicting Islam and Islamist movements as a 'global threat' that
> must be curbed. Further, they have argued that the Muslim world
> in general and middle Eastern and North African countries in par-
> ticular are unable to embrace the nature of modern human
> progress, namely individual freedoms, democratic governance,
> social tolerance, women's rights and political competition.[1]

In the vigorous discourse about the interplay of East and West,
Samuel Huntingdon propounded a defining view of this
"clash of civilizations". He argued that the world was at the
dawn of a new world order in which wars of politics and ideology have yielded to the war of cultures:

> Local politics is the politics of ethnicity; global politics is the poli-
> tics of civilizations. The rivalry of the superpowers is replaced by
> the clash of civilizations ... and the most dangerous cultural con-
> flicts are those along the fault lines between civilizations.[2]

The fault lines of conflict and civil war stretch across the continents where these civilizations meet, and they are especially clear along the boundary looping across Eurasia and Africa that separates Muslims and non-Muslims. In Africa this cuts right through nations like Nigeria and the Sudan, both with Islamic northern regions and Christian/animist southern sections. War and aggression mark the points of contact. Elsewhere, Huntingdon points to a "Tehran-Islamabad-Beijing axis" that is bent on counterbalancing Western economic and military might, with the "swing" civilizations joining the Western Alliance.[3]

Huntingdon's important thesis of the clash of civilizations is open to critique for underestimating nationalism and other factors. It nevertheless attempts to explain that global politics has shifted from an interaction of nations to a stand-off between the broader entities of civilizations.[4] The fault line of this antagonism may include national boundaries, but can slice through individual states. Though it is helpful to start with this broad brush approach, a simplistic projection of monolithic Western civilization pitted against a monolithic Islamic civilization must be avoided.

Any thoughtful response to Islamism must take Muslim diversity extremely seriously and avoid religious and socio-political reductionism. This is a caveat that Rushdie issues:

> This is not wholly to go along with Samuel Huntingdon's thesis about the clash of civilizations, for the simple reason that the Islamists' project is turned not only against the West and 'the Jews,' but also against their fellow Islamists. Whatever the public rhetoric, there's little love lost between the Taliban and Iranian regimes. Dissensions between Muslim nations run at least as deep, if not deeper, than those nations' resentment of the West.[5]

The complexities of the Muslim community are crucial for understanding Islamic civilization and political expression. Geographic and sectarian differences are compounded by ethnic divisions, poverty, affluence and education. It is difficult to unravel the theology of the "Islamist" without understanding the socio-political determinants of what is, in effect, *theology in action*. We have seen this in the rise of the Taliban, which cannot be properly understood in political isolation apart from issues such as oil, the Cold War, tribalism and the drug trade – all of which contributed to Afghani Islamic self-understanding.

That there is no monolithic Islam means that Western powers can be allied with certain Muslim states and be united in military action against other Muslim powers. In recent years, particularly with regards to public perception in times of war and aggression, it has been essential that a coalition formed between allies from Islamic and Western states be perceived as a "coalition against Iraq" or "against terrorism" – so that it is not seen as Western aggression against Islam. A stark West/Islam confrontation would, in propaganda terms, play into the hands of Islamist groups trying to nurture the power of pan-Islamist sentiments.

In the early stages of the 2001/2 international action in Afghanistan, the broadcasts of the Al Qaeda network appealed to Islamic solidarity in the face of a multinational alliance which included the support, and even co-operation, of many Muslim states. This is a powerful appeal by Al Qaeda to worldwide Muslim allegiance to the *Umma* – the global Islamic community – over and above other cultural and national allegiances. In response, other governments have sought to frustrate attempts to foster an anti-Western Islamic solidarity, believing that a clash of civilizations could only yield devastating results. Thus, for a variety of pragmatic, economic and political reasons, a state's allegiance to Islam does not, and probably never has, generated a homogenous response to world events.

The Political Nature of Islam

In analyzing the causes of Islamism, Monshipouri helpfully identifies a victim mentality, as a reaction to the ideas and political reality of the West. This victim phenomenon has come partly in response to the power of global capitalism and partly from the effects of empire and colony. Colonialism left a legacy that shapes much of Islamic-West relations – any contemporary understanding must take this colonial history seriously. Both Pakistan and Jordan owe their inception to a British colonial context. Even after independence had been successfully achieved, lingering symbiosis affected specific cases of Islamic militancy – where, for example, colonial support for a particular religious or ethnic subsection of society fuelled religious fervour among the disenfranchised.

When world events make an Islamic state seem like a victim (take, for example, Iraq), the collective memory of crusades and colonialism can generate a sense of injustice as the wronged victim feels the need to rise up against the evil of the oppressing Western powers. Muslim glory, power and self-confidence declined considerably after the Renaissance.[6] When dealing with the West, many Muslims feel that they are operating from a position of weakness and vulnerability. Islamic states that assist the West do not let Islam down, but are seen as those who have come under evil influence, namely the power of the West or America. It is thus easier in these contexts for certain "reforming" Islamist groups to rally support for their cause. Islam can then become the culture and motivating "language of dissent", thereby providing religiously emotive credentials to what may have originally been an internal ethnic or political struggle for power. In Algeria, for instance, the Islamists gained support from the marginalized urban masses (mostly displaced traditional and rural communities) and mobilized action against the Francophile elite upon whom a corrupt post-colonial regime was founded. Active Western support for that regime, which in this case was French, meant that internal politics of dissent also had to contend with the power of a Western nation.[7]

Salman Rushdie, exemplar of the Islamic/West tension, rebuts those who want to lay *all* the blame for extreme forms of Islam on this dynamic with the West:

Twenty years ago, when I was writing a novel about power struggles in a fictionalized Pakistan, it was already *de rigueur* in the

Muslim world to blame all its troubles on the West and, in particular, the United States. Then as now, some of these criticisms were
well-founded; no room here to rehearse the geopolitics of the cold
war and America's frequently damaging foreign policy 'tilts', to
use the Kissinger term, toward (or away from) this or that temporarily useful (or disapproved-of) nation-state, or America's role
in the installation and deposition of sundry unsavory leaders and
regimes. But I wanted then to ask a question that is no less important now: Suppose we say that the ills of our societies are not
primarily America's fault, that we are to blame for our own fail-
ings? How would we understand them then? Might we not, by
accepting our own responsibility for our problems, begin to learn
to solve them for ourselves?[8]

Rushdie's question is one that the Taliban in fact asked and
attempted to answer in their version of Islam. They felt that
Islam had deep shortcomings due to the failure of Islamic
regimes to fully implement *Shariah* law. The Taliban felt able to
criticize the previous expression of Islam in Afghanistan for its
"tainting" by Western culture and philosophy, and they were
seeking a return to "pure" Islam.[9]

Perhaps the best way to secure the peaceful coexistence of
Islam and the West would be to "de-politicize" Islam, thereby
curbing the political effect of so-called "extremist" Islamic
groups. We do not have space to explore the impact of secularism on religion in the West, and its philosophical and pragmatic
effect on Islam, but it is still useful to ask here whether Islam can
be separated from its political expression.[10] There are very good
reasons for arguing that there is a fusion of political life and faith
at the heart of Islam that cannot be denied without denying central aspects of this faith. We have already mentioned many of
these aspects, which are summarized below:

● **The political identity of early Islam** – Muhammad and the
  earliest followers of Islam existed as a political community
  from their conception, and much of the *Hadith* supports
  this view. Muhammad was involved not only in military
  action, and the conquest of Mecca itself, but also in the

judiciary of Medina, as he arbitrated in political and civil disputes.

- **The Qur'an** – The Qur'an intertwines law and narrative theology. For example, Sura 7 includes eschatology, narrative, prophetic passages and passages about the Jews. Sura 4 includes legal passages about women, purification rites, eschatology, narrative and teachings about Christ.

- **Commitment** – Though Muslims speak of hypocrisy, apostasy and heresy, it has been highly unusual to encounter a concept of "nominalism" within. There is no distinction between a "visible" and "invisible" Islamic community. And, in popular Islam, observance of the five pillars, or even uttering the bismillah (the basic sentence of faith), is enough for one to be termed a Muslim. The outward observance of Islamic ritual is sufficient. Detractors from this idea can be found especially amongst the Sufi, who many regard as unorthodox.[11]

- **Shariah** – Although *Shariah* law is theoretically binding only to Muslims, where an Islamic state adopts *Shariah* there is seldom any real space for non-Muslims to carry out their own faith in freedom. They are free, rather, to practise "within the bounds of Islamic law". This has significant ramifications in terms of the blasphemy law and conversion to other religions – both of which can carry the death penalty. Under *Shariah* law all minority religious groups must pay Jizya (a higher tax), which legally enforces a religious apartheid. In court, a non-Muslim can be convicted with only one Muslim witness, though the converse is not legal, and this has led to significant abuse of minority women.[12] *Shariah* provides a poor framework for Muslims living within non-Islamic states, which makes cultural assimilation in the West more difficult.

The clash of civilizations highlights two utterly different ways of understanding the world, and particularly the interaction of religion and politics. In stark contrast to most Islamic thought, the de-politicization or secularization of religion has become so ingrained in Western thought that it is often assumed that religion and politics are necessarily a potent mix. Many Muslim nations, by contrast, take for granted that Islam cannot exist apolitically, and they take steps to work within the world-view of the Muslim to ensure that religious discourse does not lead to civil unrest or revolution.

We consider two very different case studies of politics and religion in Jordan and Algeria.

CASE STUDY: Jordan – Controlling Islamic Discourse and Practice

Jordan is actively involved in "Muslim politics", for it is one of many states that relies to some extent upon Islam for its legitimacy. Both the state and the royal family have vested interests in establishing and maintaining these links with Islam, and in influencing Islamic discourse in favour of the state. Because Islam is inherently political, little religious dialogue can take place without political implications. Threats to the stability of an Islamic regime frequently emerge from religious discourse, and political challenges are often vocalized in religious language. It has been important to the Jordanian administration, therefore, to influence certain voices within this discourse – raising some to prominence, and muting others.

The Hashemites in the Transjordan were granted state formation (i.e. Jordan) in return for supporting Britain against the Ottoman Empire in World War I. Abdullah, the grandfather of King Hussein, became leader of this new territory which at that time was dominated by a multitude of independent tribes with little or no loyalty to their new Hashemite ruler. Because of the British support for the kingdom, it was crucial that the Islamic credentials of the new dynasty be emphasized in order to quell dissent. The Hashemites therefore emphasized their genealogical connection to the prophet Muhammad (they are from the same Quryashi tribe); their historic connection with

Islamic sites (their ancestors ruled Mecca from 1201 to 1925); and the fact that Abdullah I was shot and killed at al-Aqsa mosque in Jerusalem in 1951 – which gives the family the aura of martyrdom.[13]

At a speech given at the amendment of election law in 1993 Hussein stated:

> I call upon you all to realize that the Arab Hashemite Hussein, who has been honoured by the Almighty Allah to be a descendent of the prophet Mohammad bin Abdullah, peace be upon him, is above all worldly titles and positions.[14]

The Jordanian government seeks to regulate Islamic discourse in a number of ways – in relation to the mosque, the Friday sermon (*khutba*) and the right of Imams to teach and minister. The mosque is multifunctional, and reactionary groups have frequently used it as a base for their support – especially in organizing demonstrations after the Friday sermon. Although, as we have seen, the Friday sermon is meant to be a comment on contemporary issues and politics from an Islamic point of view, a dose of rhetoric and indignation can often ignite an unsettled congregation. Throughout the Muslim world there is often a distinction made between "official" mosques and "private" mosques, the latter of which are not regulated by the state. Egypt is attempting to discourage the private mosques in order to retain some influence on the content of the sermons, but has thus far failed to do so. Jordan has been more successful and legally all mosques, whether official or private, come under government control. One commentator writes: "This control … produces a docile version of Islam that reifies state power and prevents critical elements from utilizing this space to disseminate an alternative interpretation of meaning."[15] The mosque in Jordan carries out many community functions such as marriage, debate and arbitration of local disputes, and the Friday sermon is meant to make connections with the social and political issues of the day.

In Jordan the Imams, who are local leaders of congregational prayers and Qur'anic instruction, givers of the Friday sermon, and in overall control of the life and rituals of the mosque, are selected and controlled by a process that is closely monitored by the government. On completing their training, Imams are considered to be civil servants and are hired under the civil servant laws as government employees. Government selection processes choose "balanced thinkers" who will not be critical of policies, and they consciously avoid choosing radical thinkers, or preachers who would be critical of the state. After selection, the observation and training of the Imams continues throughout their careers, through the Centre for the Rehabilitation of Imams. Particular attention is paid to the *khutba*, whose content must be written down each week, and whose topic is often prescribed.[16] These measures are largely successful at limiting the dissenting potential of the mosques, though many of these processes are not as efficient as they sound and are hindered by the shortage of qualified Imams in the country.

Jordan has therefore largely managed to discourage "radical" Islamic movements by recognizing the essentially political nature of Islamic theology and manipulating this to serve the stability of the state.

CASE STUDY: Algerian Islamism – a Different Answer to the Religious Sphere

Although Algerian Islamism is fairly diverse, and follows specific mosques or preachers, Hugh Roberts argues that it gathers around several unifying aims, which sum up the purpose of da'wa, the call to live Islamically. The first is to assert the autonomy of the religious sphere, and to wrestle free from government control of religious activities and beliefs. This has been done by setting up independent, or "free" mosques. In Algerian law a mosque automatically comes under government control once the building has been finished. So by the early 1980s there were over two thousand "unfinished" mosques that were fully functioning. Imams in these mosques could ignore sermon outlines and guidelines, and are dependent on local contributions, rather than on a government salary. Some say that this made the Friday sermons better.

The long-term aim of the Islamists is a pure Islamic state, by which is meant "a state governed in accordance with the Sharia". Roberts writes:

> Islamic law, being divine in origin and therefore immutable (unchangeable), presupposes a state in which the executive is subordinate to the judiciary, and the judiciary operate within the parameters defined by the Ulama. In such a state the legislature has only a very secondary role, since innovative law-giving is by definition un-Islamic, and ruled out. The Islamic state is thus a state in which the religious sphere has primacy over the political sphere.[17]

A second theme in Algerian Islamism is the vigorous engagement in the censoring of morality (*hisba*). This has been done through mobilizing groups to take action, usually through intimidation, against those who have "immodest dress", or seem to be engaging in "decadent" cultural practices imported from outside authentic Islam, such as ostentatious eating and risqué theatre. The most visible expression of this revolution of moral censorship comes in terms of women's dress – the Iranian cultural dress of the chador replacing the more delicate Algerian *haik* – a thin, translucent veil. The third theme that Roberts brings out is the opposition to the Algerian "left". Opposition to radical socialist and communist groups in politics and academia, also seen in Palestine, helps the emergent groups to define both "boundaries" in their social and political struggle for Islamic society. One boundary is set against lacklustre and compromising religion, and the other against social reform without Islam on the other. These three themes inspired recourse to violence by Islamist mobs, and reached their height in 1980–82. Radical Islamic groups then joined the process of elections from 1989 by joining the political party system.

What is most important in Algeria, in contrast to the Jordanian question, is the issue of whether the "religious sphere" is subservient to the "political". Prior to 1990 Islamists worked outside the political system, censoring morality through intimidation rather than legislation. This demonstrated on the streets their reluctance to accept the concept of political sovereignty over the religious realm. Free mosques are also visible signs of this attempt by religious groupings to escape government control and censorship, or even direction.

Is Islamic Militancy a Threat to the West?

In exploring the clash of civilizations between the West and Islam, we have seen that neither civilization is monolithic, that the religion of Islam tends towards full political engagement, the excesses of which are seen in the vibrant Islamist movements across the world. The authentic fusion of politics and religion in Islam is an essential difference of approach from that of the West and is a significant factor in understanding any tension that may occur.

Several Western governments have identified the increasing threat that Islamism poses to the safety of individuals in the West and even to the democratic way of life. Western leaders have begun to appeal to a global ethic – a universally recognized set of views and values, which are shared by Western powers, and can be maintained as true in every culture. This is problematic because while these values may be good and true, the historic suspicions and grievances within the Islamic civilization, and a sense of victimization, make it difficult for reform to come from outside. The militant, violent, radical Muslims, who pose a threat to the world, would most successfully be dealt with by other members of the Islamic community. Ideally the Umma must reform itself. The clash of civilizations will only become more dangerous if this does not happen, and the Islamists succeed in carrying the rest of the Muslim world along with their agenda.

Anti-globalization riots demonstrate that some of the Islamic critiques of Western culture are passionately shared by other social reformers, Marxists and libertarians. The rampant materialism of unbridled capitalism is not without its victims, especially in the Third World. Muslims are not alone in criticizing the West for its decadence – the cultural historian Jacques Barzun thinks that this is a fair description: "When people accept futility and the absurd is normal the culture is decadent. The term is not a slur, it is a technical label."[18] Many Muslim militants are deeply committed to the destruction of the decadent Western civilization, others are determined to see the establishment of *Shariah* law in every country where there is a Muslim community. However, free speech and fatwas are not easy bedfellows.

If Islamic groups choose to express their opposition to the subservience of the religious sphere to the political, and to do so through non-democratic means, then this may be a threat to Western norms. That a small minority have chosen to embrace violence within Britain, is illustrated by Richard Reid, the "shoe bomber from Brixton" who was recruited from prison by an extremist group, to blow up a plane as part of *jihad*.[19] The West must articulate the ideas and values it seeks to defend and in so doing recognize that where any value or ideal is upheld, its antithesis cannot also be valid. The militant Islamic critique shows that absolute pluralism itself cannot be maintained. The flourishing of Islamism across the world, and the ability of Islamic terrorist networks to use the technology, travel, transport, weapons and communications to subvert the same technological society which gave them birth, shows that there are gaping holes of vulnerability in Western society.

---

[1] Monshipouri, *The West's Encounter with Islam*, p. 3.

[2] Huntingdon, *The Clash of Civilizations*, p. 29.

[3] Huntingdon, *Clash*, p. 240.

[4] Walt criticizes Huntingdon's assumption that similar cultures necessarily maintain peace or that differing cultures are incapable of peaceful coexistence. Walt, *Building up New Bogeymen*, pp. 177–89.

[5] Rushdie in the *New York Times*, 2 November. 2001.

[6] Fuller and Lesser, *A Sense of Siege: The Geopolitics of Radical Islam and the West*, pp. 17–19; 27–31.

7   Monshipouri, *The West's Encounter with Islam*, p. 9. See also Khurshid Ahmad, *Islam and the West: Confrontation or Cooperation?*, pp. 63–81.

8   Rushdie in the *New York Times*, 2 November 2001.

9   Though the Taliban are a cultural backlash against what they see as Western influences in Afghanistan, much of what they articulate as "pure" Islam could in fact be understood as Pashtun cultural practices and assumptions. The burka is a case in point, as is their total rejection of images of every kind. Both of these find some support in *Hadith* and the Qur'an – but the specific expressions of the practices now enforced throughout the nation by *Shariah* law are fairly particular to the Pashtuns.

10 Newbigin, *Gospel and the pluralist society*. Paul Badham, ed., *Religion, state and society in modern Britain*, Edwin Mellen Press, New York, 1989. M.E. Hamdi, *The Politicisation of Islam: Essays on Democratic Governance*. Westview Press, Oxford, 1998. Paul Beaumont, ed., *Christian Perspectives on Law Reform*, Paternoster, Carlisle, 1998. David Wells, *God in the Wasteland*, IVP, Leicester, 1994.

11 See chapter 1.

12 See Appendix.

13 Wiktorowicz, *State Power and the Regulation of Islam in Jordan*, p. 3.

14 Hussein, *Selected Speeches by His Majesty King Hussein*, p. 91.

15 Wiktorowicz, *State Power*, p. 6.

16 Wiktorowicz, *State Power*, p. 10. In the past, the government has suggested discussion on topics as specific as traffic and car fatalities.

17 Roberts, Hugh, *Algerian Islamism*, p. 444–5.

18 Barzun, *Dawn to Decadence*, p. 11.

19 *Daily Telegraph*, 22 December 2001.

6

Avenues for a Christian Response

A good man was ther of religioun,
That was a povre Persoun of a toun,
But riche he was of hooly thoght and werk.
He was also a lerned man, a clerk,
That Cristes gospel trewely wolde preche …
This noble ensample to his sheep he yaf,
That first he wroghte, and afterward he taughte …
A bettre preest I trowe that nowher noon ys.
He waited after no pompe and reverence,
Ne maked him a spiced conscience,
But Cristes loore and his apostles twelve
He taughte; but first he folwed it hymselve.

Chaucer *The Canterbury Tales*, Prologue, 477–81, 496–97, 524–28

Because Christianity predates Islam by so many years, there
has been interaction, co-operation and misunderstanding
between the two religions in varying intensity since the time of
Muhammad. Neither Christians nor Muslims have understood
their own way of life in cultural abstraction, and so politics,
culture and economics of the faiths have frequently been intertwined. Although there are many examples of peaceful and
fruitful interaction between the two faith communities, the
numerous crusades, and particularly the sackings of Jerusalem,
are impossible to ignore. To this day the crusades are important
in shaping Islamic self-understanding, for they represent the

cruelty of Christian cultural imperialism. The ancient grievance remains at the front of contemporary Islamic consciousness, and Muslim apologists have been known to cite it when Islamic militancy is critiqued. The widespread and vocal reaction to President Bush's use of the language of "crusade" in the early days of American military action against Afghanistan in 2001 has brought the prevalence of these sensitivities to light.

Religious hatred is often blamed for war, suffering and violence, and there are numerous examples of wars fought with religious justification. The twentieth century, however, paints a slightly different picture. The combined efforts of Nazism and Communism, both atheistic philosophies, have been responsible for far more cruelty and bloodshed than many thought could ever be possible. This said, the medieval use of faith as a tool of military oppression and imperialism is more than regrettable. It leaves a bitter taste in the mouth of all Christians, whether or not both sides perpetrated cruelty, or regardless of whose barbarism outstripped whose. For theological analysis, and in an attempt to provide a Christian response, we must ask whether the military expression of faith was an outworking of those faith systems, a corruption of them, or even the antithesis of what they stand for. For the Christian a biblical and Christ-like approach to Islamic militancy will ask questions of its own history and will examine what a true Christian response should look like.

The early crusades

The history of the crusading era is as fascinating as it is complicated. Much of the history is accessible to us through highly charged documents, which are rich in poetry and are intended as propoganda. The wars took place over several hundred years of shifting politics and started in the eleventh century, when the Middle East was already a turbulent mosaic of warring factions.

In the Middle East during the eleventh century the Sunni community was largely represented by the Seljuks. From 1038, the Seljuk sultans had pretended to rule as the servants of the Abbasid Caliph, and to uphold Sunni Islam on their behalf. In reality, the caliphs had little real power, even in Baghdad, though they remained the official visible heads of the religious and political Sunni Islamic world.

The Shi'ites, who had already split into a number of important subgroups, were mixed in among the other Muslims – though the Shi'ite understanding of political and religious allegiance differed considerably from that of the other Muslims. All Shi'ites believed that political and spiritual authority could only be held by Ali and his descendants, the Imams. The term "Shi'ite" is taken from "Shi'a Ali", which means "the supporters of Ali" (Muhammad's son-in-law). Within the Shi'ite community, the "Twelvers" waited for the return of the twelfth Imam, who was believed to have disappeared in the year 878 and would return to establish Islamic justice in the whole world. Another group, the Isma'ilis, argued that Isma'il, the seventh Imam, was the last authentic Imam, and they did not recognize the spiritual authenticity of any other Imam after his "disappearance" in 760. Other breakaway groups included the Druze and the Nizari Isma'ilis (known as the Assassins), who broke away and later opposed the Fatimid caliphate in Cairo. Geographically, the Islamic community also spread into what is now modern Europe, with particular power in Spain and Sicily.

The Middle Eastern mosaic also included a significant Christian minority. The Orthodox (known as Melkites) looked to the Byzantine emperor for leadership and protection. Many Jacobite, Nestorian and Maronite groups, however, who were essentially Eastern, had little or no allegiance either to Byzantine political authority or to the Western Church. Some Egyptian Copts even held high ranks in the armed forces of the Fatimid caliphs. The changing influence of the Nestorian church illustrates this religious flux. Although the Nestorian church had declined enormously by this period, it formed a backdrop to many of the early Islamic advances into Central Asia, for several centuries heavily Christianized through the Nestorians.

The warring between Sunni and Shi'ite power bases, and even within these sects, formed part of the Middle Eastern context of the eleventh century. The most significant feature in the run-up to the first crusade was the rapid collapse of the Seljuk Empire, which unravelled with infighting during the late eleventh and early twelfth centuries, as rival warlords and heirs scrabbled for influence and power. One historian comments that, "In the late eleventh century Greater Syria was a vast war zone fought over by generals and former clients of the Seljuks on the one hand and armies in the service of the Fatimid Caliphs of Egypt on the other."[1]

The danger faced by pilgrims in Palestine, though authentic in such an unstable political situation, does not seem to be the real reason for the first crusade. Rather, the territorial gains made at the expense of the Greeks in Asia Minor by a Seljuk Sultan, Kilij Arslan I, led the Byzantine emperor, Alexius I, to ask for military help from the West. The ensuing victories of the Franks hardly seem surprising amidst such turmoil. Different Islamic factions had fought fiercely over Jerusalem, and it had already changed hands from Shi'ite to Sunni and back to the Shi'ite Fatimids again between 1071 and 1098. So when the Franks captured the city on 15 July 1099, they were mistaken as Byzantine forces, and many of the Sunnis viewed the collapse of the city with a quiet satisfaction that their own enemies, the Shi'ites, had been defeated.[2] The capture of Jerusalem also coincided with a plague in Egypt that temporarily weakened the Egyptian regime, which confidently expected to take the city back within the year.

The full significance of Jerusalem having passed out of Islamic hands took a few years to sink in. Indeed, in 1110, 11 years after the fall of Jerusalem, and despite the capture or killing of the Muslim inhabitants of that city by the Franks, no retaliatory response whatsoever had been mustered. The year 1110 is significant in that it marked a demonstration in Baghdad to raise Sunni support for the rebuttal of the Franks, but it amounted to nothing. Between the 1140s and the 1160s we can see significant renewed interest in *jihad* as a religious motivation for regaining Palestinian territory, and this was generated in the Madrassahs, and in various religious tracts, such as Bahr al-Fava'id. Only when the warlord Saladin came to power in Egypt (1171) and in Damascus (1174) was there a significant leader in the region who had the ability to unite any forces against the Franks (who had by this stage been in Jerusalem for about 75 years). Jerusalem fell to Saladin on 2 October 1187, after which he argued that this "end" (of capturing the "brother city of Mecca") justified the "means" (of subduing and waging war against fellow Muslims for the whole of his career up until that point).[3] Jerusalem remained under the caliphate until a treaty handed it back into Frankish control in 1229.

The to-ing and fro-ing of Jerusalem illustrates that contemporary attempts to point to Christian cruelty during the crusades as a justification for contemporary Islamic aggression fails to embrace the complex political and religious mosaic that formed the backdrop to Islamic-Western aggression during that period, and moreover fails to appreciate the intense sectarian hatred that existed within Islam itself. That "forces of the cross" displayed terrible cruelty is undeniable, but these were always in the context of the aggression and cruelty of warfare that was common to the era, and were not distinct from internecine warfare among "Christian" or "Muslim" forces.

The crusading past of the Christian church is one of the greatest tragedies of church history – that the popes ever saw fit to declare war in Christ's name on Muslims, or for that matter on fellow Christian peoples, has been rightly condemned as an aberration of the Christian gospel for several centuries. The same cannot be said of many sectors of the Islamic community, for whom *jihad*, in all its senses, still retains its potency.

Even at the time, true Christian voices spoke up for biblical and Christ-like faith. The thoughts and actions of Francis of Assisi and the early Franciscan monks demonstrate that despite the Papal unfaithfulness to the Gospel during the crusades, true Christianity was never completely eclipsed. The life of Francis is notoriously difficult to unravel from hagiography, yet the peace-loving, evangelistic attitude of Francis demonstrates adherence to the biblical exhortations to follow Christ's example. The Franciscan behaviour towards the Sultan and his Muslim crusaders struck a deep chord and impacted many Christians and Muslims at the time. Christine Mallouhi writes: "The story of the monk and the Sultan is one intriguing link in the chain of amazing encounters and friend-ships leaping across the chasm of brutality during the Crusade wars."[4] It appears that during a short truce in the battle for the control of Damietta in the summer of 1219, Francis and some of his monks, who had travelled to the front to preach the gospel and speak for peace, made use of the opportunity to cross the lines and speak to the Muslims camped there. The crusaders "must have been totally flabbergasted that he intended to preach the very same message to the Muslims that he had preached to the crusaders themselves. The same mes-sage for those infidels as for the believers."[5]

As Christians reflect on this today, and seek to respond to Islam, it becomes clear that even in the midst of the evil and brutality of the crusades a true Christian response did not take up arms but peaceably approached all human beings with an offer of the gospel. This follows the pattern of Christ who renounced violence and coercion in favour of healing, teach-ing and evangelizing. On many occasions Jesus himself was encouraged to take up arms to further his cause. The tri-umphal entry into Jerusalem was on the back of a donkey – a peace-loving domestic animal, not a horse of war – and at his arrest Christ rebuked Peter for cutting the ear off of one of the arresting party. Even in the contemporary context of the per-secution of Christians by Muslims around the world, this same approach of peaceful faith sharing is followed.

A Christian Critique of Militarized Faith

Any attempt to militarize the church, as various popes have ventured to do, is more than an unwise mistake. It is the direct antithesis of Christianity, cutting across the life and teaching of

Christ, the Christian Holy Scriptures and the practice of the early Church. A good example of a true Christian approach in example and theology comes from the writings of John Wyclif. Even in the era of a church institution embroiled in war and violence and ambitious in the realm of politics, Wycliffe provided a prophetic voice, calling Christian believers back to the true faith. Forged by the scriptures, eager for the gospel message to go forth and faithful to the person and work of Christ, Wycliffe wrote helpfully against militarizing the church.

Wycliffe was born in about 1324 near the village of Wycliffe in Yorkshire. Like many scholars and clerics of his day, he spent much of his life in Oxford, where he was a student at Balliol college, and later was Master there. Later in his life, he was sidelined to relative obscurity and was given a parish in Lutterworth from 1374 until his death of a stroke on 29 December 1384. These brief details belie the impact of the man dismissed in his day as a heretic, and later dubbed the "Morning Star of the Reformation" for his prefiguring of many of the reforms that were to follow in Europe during the Reformation itself.

It comes as a surprise to many readers today that several aspects of the critical stance of the European reformers towards the abuses of the medieval church owe much of their inspiration to previous works handed down to them by Hussite and Lollard scholars and writers. Luther, for example, wrote a preface to a commentary on Revelation and wholeheartedly recommends the treatise sent to him "by the most eminent scholars from the border regions of Germany":

> Understand therefore, good readers that we have written this preface to make known to all, wherever they live, that we are not the first to interpret the papacy as the rule of Antichrist ... This author ... [is] a witness preordained by God for the confirmation of our doctrine so many years before us.[6]

The work is not a German treatise, however, as Luther supposed, but a continental copy of the Lollard work "Opus

Arduum". The Lollards, in turn, had received much of their interpretative stance from Wycliffe.[7]

Particularly important for us here was Wycliffe's conviction that true Christians should not have a militarized faith because it betrays the teachings and example of Christ and the apostles and is contrary to the teaching of Scripture. He was a reformer who maintained that Scripture had greater authority than the church or human reason in matters of faith, conduct and understanding. He translated the (Latin) Bible into English and uttered stern rebukes to the military and ecclesiastical hierarchy of the era.

Wycliffe felt that a root and branch reappraisal of the Roman Catholic church was needed. The church and ecclesiastical community had become so corrupt that they were the exact antithesis of what faith in Christ was meant to be. In a letter to Pope Urban VI, Wycliffe argued that just as James and John "erred when they coveted worldly high-ness", so any Christian who hungers after that kind of power errs in the same way. He went even further and appealed directly to the pope to give up his imperial power – "to leave his worldly lordship to worldly lordis", and to encourage all his clergy to do the same. Moreover, he argued that this is what Christ did and what he taught his disciples to do, and that those ecclesiastics who by abusing their power persist in "error against god's law ... are open heretics".[8] He hoped that the pope would take the initiative, give up his military and colonial power, and concentrate on preaching the gospel and serving, rather than ruling, his people and encouraging a wider range of abuses. He feared however that the stand of the medieval church would persist, and that the pope would thereby be shown to be in direct opposition to the will and law of Christ – therefore revealing himself to be the Antichrist.

This shouldn't be understood today as anti-Catholic bigotry. That would be an anachronism, for Wycliffe was a Catholic priest himself and predated the Reformation by several generations. His conception of "Antichrist" here means "opposed to Christ and his law". This is not the same as the personalized excesses of later years that would be illustrated in the sixteenth-century Protestant woodcuts of Cranach. Rather, the pope is the figurehead of a system and a body politic that directly oppose the cause and the attributes of the Christian church, while still bearing the name and claiming to be the authentic church in Europe. The military monks, as well as indulgences sold to finance the crusades, were both signs of the degeneration of the church.

Wycliffe was no wild apocalyptic herald, even though his polemic against the established church led him to expound on prophetic biblical passages and on figures associated with the end times. He documented and quantified the abuses he saw in his own day by comparing current evils with prophecies in Scripture. Over the course of his disputes with schismatic popes and intransigent theologians, Wycliffe became convinced that the Roman Catholic Church hierarchy had fallen prey to a diabolical conspiracy. Eschatological language, i.e. the language of anti-Christ, is used as an index of the enormity of the transgressions that Wycliffe has uncovered.

Wycliffe also made the point that forces opposed to God can in fact operate through those in religious service, and he cited Jesus' rebuke of Peter: "Jesus turned and said to Peter, 'Get behind me, Satan! You are a stumbling-block to me; you do not have in mind the things of God, but the things of men.'"[9] William Swyndersby, one of Wycliffe's followers, made a similar comparison and argued that no clergyman should resort to the use of the sword:

> For then I say, if the Pope holde men of armes in mayntenyng of his temporal lordeschip to venge him on hem that gylten and offenden hym … not putynge his swerde in his schethe, as God commanded to Petre, he is Anticryst.[10]

In 1383, Pope Urban ordered a crusade against his rival, and Bishop Henry Despenser of Norwich led an expedition from England into Flanders – which ended a few months later in a somewhat inglorious collapse. The warring elements in the church and this tussle for power and land clearly demonstrated to Wycliffe the church's abandonment of Christianity, and he made use of the opportunity to write one of his most effective tracts. *The Crusade* denounces the perversion of Christianity evidenced in abandoning the sacred mission and taking up the purposes of a war – started by means of prodigal offers of indulgence and sustained by the greed for plunder and the morally inexcusable yet inveterate hatred of Englishmen for France.[11]

This theology is very significant – not only for those leading the institution of the church, but also for laypeople. Although Wycliffe was not an outright pacifist, in one of his sermons on the Lord's Prayer he did warn those who fight out of vengeance that their actions have no spiritual merit, and that they are actually in danger of calling the wrath of God on their own heads. He concentrated on the Christian prayer "forgive us our debts as we forgive those who are debtors against us" and commented that though forgiveness is not conditional, as such, there is a reciprocity involved. Forgive us, as we forgive. If men are at war, and showing no signs of forgiveness but rather anger and revenge, then that is like asking for the same from the hand of God. Thus he advised the crusading armies that they were better off saying nothing than praying such a prayer.[12] This was a stern rebuttal to those who wanted to make use of Christianity in the cause of war, coming from a plain explanation of the biblical text. The teaching was specifically directed against those who applied a spiritual/religious veneer to what was in fact a war for power, control, greed and territory.

Wycliffe and Islam

Though the main crusade in Wycliffe's day was being waged between two papal parties, he did refer to the clash of Christendom and Islam in his biblical commentaries. He was a keen and useful political thinker, and many of his commentaries seem to have one eye on the turbulent events of his time, from which he observed that things did not bode well for the church. It seemed to him that the biblical prophets warned that the corrupt church would suffer affliction at the hands of the Antichrist in the last days. Wycliffe charged the medieval church with fulfilling this diabolical role – seducing countless thousands, and leading them away from a true and living faith in Christ, and away from obedience to him. He argued that the authentic church had blossomed, paradoxically, as it endured tyrants' swords, whereas the peace and quiet she had enjoyed since Constantine had given rise to a flaccid church whose leaders had forsaken their fear of God and placed their confidence in material wealth.

The crusades against Islam, and particularly the ensuing defeat of "Christian" forces at the hands of Muslims does nothing to confirm the just cause of the "religious war", but rather stood as evidence of God's displeasure at the state of the medieval Western church. It was the widespread opposition to Christ in life, the abandonment of true Christian doctrine and the sinful behaviour of corrupt clerics, monks and priests, which was at fault. So rather than being the enemies of Christianity, the forces of Islam "were sent by God to punish the sinful and arrogant grasping of a church that had lost her way and then represented the antithesis of authentic Christianity."[13]

The second, and most significant, sign of Wycliffe's doctrine (and a point that was to be taken up vigorously by Michael Sattler, the Mennonites, and other evangelical Anabaptists of the European Reformation) is an even-handed attitude to Islam and imperial Christianity. Neither the visible church of his day, nor the Islamic community, was faithful in obedience to God, as neither was following Christ. Wycliffe argued that the evangelical faith, which goes back to obeying Christ and his way, was equally opposed, even persecuted, by both Muslims and medieval ecclesiastical leaders. Wycliffe linked the "widespread panic" foretold by the prophet Zechariah with the continuous war fought among nominal Christians and the internal conflict within the Muslim ranks.[14] The chaos that both communities often wrestled with was to bring them to dependence on God in and through Christ. Wycliffe's call to follow Christ was also even-handed – even though he did not, to our knowledge, particularize the missionary implications of this much further for Islam. He tended to concentrate more on the duty of the so-called Christian leaders to demonstrate their faith – if they had one – through teaching about Christ, preaching the gospel and being militant in prayer and intercession rather than in outright war.

The third issue to consider is Wycliffe's progression of thought. Although Wycliffe was even-handed towards Islam and militarized Christendom, what begins as a critique from within – a movement for reform of the Catholic church – later takes on the more radical position held in later Lollard and Anabaptist theology, and which was picked up by Luther. When interpreting the passages in Revelation and trying to analyse the biggest opponent to the Christian faith (the forces of Antichrist), Wycliffe finally fixes firmly on the papacy – and not on Islam. Wycliffe thus became convinced that counterfeit Christianity, the sham that the church had become, *was a greater opponent to the Christian faith than Islam* – the dangers of which were most clearly displayed in the West, and not in the East at all.

The implication is that the crusades cannot and must not be seen as a war between Christianity and Islam, but rather as a war between two types of militarized religion – both of which are contrary to the Christian faith. In some sense, the religious foundation of both sides was essentially the same. Both sides were equally opposed to a church that knew and communicated the gospel of Christ and was more interested in the kingdom of God than worldly authority. Wycliffe argued that the authentic response of the church should be one of continuing to share the good news of Jesus – at all times, with all people.

Is Islamic militancy a threat to Christians?

As we have seen in Chapter 5, and in the light of anthrax attacks and the appalling destruction of the World Trade

Center on 11 September, we know that terrorist groups are able to pose a threat to Western powers and the safety of individuals in the West. But we must ask if an attack on the West is really an attack on Christians. Is a threat to the West a threat to Christians, or even to Christianity per se? The current focus on Islamic self-understanding and interaction with Western values and democracy ought to encourage the Christian communities of the West to assess their own self-understanding and assimilation.

It may be tempting to connect the "West" with Christianity, yet there are many good reasons for not doing so. Apart from Christian dissent from the highly visible norms of mass Western culture, such as unbridled materialism, godlessness and immorality, it is also true that the connection may be unwise numerically speaking. Evangelical Christianity is the voice of a minority in Europe, and in Britain the numbers of those regularly attending church are comparable with those of other faith communities. The point may be made more tellingly here than in the Americas. Monshipouri contends that:

> it is no longer plausible to perceive of Christian–Muslim relations in terms of Islam and the West, because today the centres of Christianity and Islam have shifted to Africa, Asia and the Americas, and the fluid nature of modern society has led to a retreat from geographic separation.[15]

Perhaps now, more than ever, the accusation that Christianity is a Western religion can be abandoned.

So the identification of the West with Christianity is unwise both in terms of confusing contemporary Western values with Christian ethics, as well as for numerical reasons. This has another danger, in that it undermines the very real suffering of Christian minorities in other parts of the world. While it is true that Christians suffer a great deal of persecution in many nations that are not Islamic, such as in China, Islamic militancy does pose a real and physical threat in Islamic states, such as Indonesia, Sudan and Iran.

Persecution

Many organizations exist to equip the Western church to respond to this persecution, as well as to provide advocacy and assistance to those communities under great pressure. The concern of Christians for persecuted members of their own faith has been instrumental in raising awareness in the wider public and political arena of a distinctly Christian response to, and understanding of, Islam. Christian voices are keen to point out that a criticism of the abuses of some Islamic groups or political expressions is not "Islamophobia", and to this effect Baroness Cox spoke in the House of Lords on 14 September 2001:

> The term "Islamism" is widely used to denote the violent, terrorist and militaristic ideology associated with many of the conflicts in the world today, such as those in Sudan and Chechnya. In highlighting the terrorist implications of Islamism, I am not in any way promoting Islamophobia; rather, the reverse. I am trying to avert it. Unless the distinction is made clearly between the adherents of violent Islamism and the vast majority of peaceable Muslims who live in our midst, there is a real danger of a backlash against the latter based on ignorance, confusion and emotional reactions to Islamist terrorism.[16]

She then went on to draw the House's attention to the plight of religious minorities under Islamic rule in Sudan:

> Before concluding, I turn briefly to relevant international aspects of Islamist terrorism. In particular, I refer to Sudan, where the National Islamic Front took power by a military coup and holds it by the ruthless oppression of its own people. That Islamist regime represents no more than between 5 per cent and 7 per cent of the Sudanese people and is deeply loathed by the vast majority. It is waging *jihad* in its most brutal form against all who oppose it, including Muslims as well as Christians and traditional believers. It has created a toll of suffering – more than 2 million are dead and more than 5 million have been displaced. The sheer scale of that

toll of tragedy exceeds that in Rwanda, Somalia and the former Republic of Yugoslavia put together.

The NIF regime has been condemned by the United Nations Security Council for complicity with terrorism and for its vast catalogue of violations against human rights. Since beginning to exploit the huge oil reserves that have recently come on line, it has used the oil revenue to purchase even more sophisticated weapons, including helicopter gunships. There have recently been reports about it using missiles against its own people in the south. It is also carrying out a brutal, systematic and comprehensive clearance of the African peoples who live around the oil fields to an extent that must be regarded as involving ethnic cleansing. Moreover, it is committed to extending its influence and ideology beyond the borders of Sudan.

The Apostle Paul testifies to the grace of God that extends even to those who, like him, carry out with religious zeal the most appalling persecution against Christians, believing that in doing so they fulfil the will of God. In Acts 9 we read the narrative of Paul as he carried out a house-to-house policy of rounding up and persecuting the Christian believers, and even as he is "breathing out murderous threats" Jesus Christ appears to him and he is converted. From that point on he is completely devoted to proclaiming the good news of God for all humankind – Jew and Gentile, slave and free. His determination to share the good news led to numerous beatings, floggings, shipwrecks, and many persecutions – even to his own death. For those Christians suffering under similar circumstances, both Paul and the Gospels have much to say. They are to bless and pray for those who persecute them. The book of Hebrews counsels persecuted Christians to persevere and to hold onto their faith during persecution. A Christian response to Islam, therefore, coincides at this point with a Christian response to persecution under any world-view, state system or situation of violence.

In the midst of this suffering, the good news remains – even for those who perpetrate such crimes. It is up to the state to administer justice. The church is to cry for justice, but not to return the injustice. The Christian conviction has always been that God listens to the oppressed and will ultimately punish the perpetrators of evil – even if they are seen to "get away with it" in the short-term of their lifetimes. Perhaps this is best expressed in the words of one commentator writing to the Russian government after the publication of *The Gulag Archipelago*, Solzhenitsyn's book uncovering the abuses of Stalin's murderous Gulags. The book was instrumental in bringing this cry for justice to the ears of the wider world:

> Some of you may begin to ask yourself; and is there over all of us one who will demand a full reckoning? Never doubt it – there is. He will demand a reckoning and you will answer … Take Russia out of the hands of Cain, and give her back to God.[17]

---

[1] Irwin, *Islam and the Crusades*, p. 217.

[2] Irwin, pp. 218–9.

[3] Irwin, p. 235.

[4] Mallouhi, *Waging Peace on Islam*, p. 263, explores this story in greater depth, and concentrates on its relevance for Christian–Islamic relations today.

[5] Mallouhi, p. 267. There are some accounts which suggest that the Sultan was persuaded by Francis' preaching of the gospel and converted to Christianity, but though it seems fairly certain that the incident of Francis sharing the good news did take place, and that he left again amicably, the evidence of conversion is flimsy and unlikely.

[6] 'Commentarius in Apocalypsin ante Centum Annos aeditus'. See also Aston, *Lollardy and the Reformation*, p. 227.

[7] Bostick, *The AntiChrist and the Lollards*, p. 55.

[8] Wycliffe, *Select English Writings*, p. 75.

[9] Matthew 16:23.

[10] Wycliffe, *Writings*, p. 113. This was a written defence handed to the Bishop of Hereford on 3 October 1391. See also Wycliffe, *De Oficio Regis*, ch. 12.

[11] Poole, *Wycliffe and Movements for Reform*, p. 100.

[12] Wycliffe, sermon, 'The Fyfth Sondai Gospel after Eester'.

[13] Bostick, *The AntiChrist*, p. 69, citing Wycliffe, 'De Christo et Anticristo' 2:673, pp. 18–20. It is easy to confuse Wycliffe's terms in today's language. The nominal church is represented by the papacy, and is involved in the crusades, whereas the authentic Christian church, which is mixed into the visible or nominal church, and opposed by it, is described as the church militant. Put simply, the militant church is the opposite of the military church.

[14] Bostick, *The AntiChrist*, p. 57 citing Wycliffe, 'Postilla super Totam Bibliam'.

[15] Monshipouri, *The West's Encounter with Islam*, p. 14.

[16] Hansard column 39/40, 14 September 2001.

[17] Pearce, *Solzhenitsyn: A Soul in Exile*, p. 216.

7

Final Thoughts

Islam is a diverse and complex religion. The concentration of some Muslim scholars on the unity of the worldwide Islamic community, or *Umma*, can obscure the different factions and streams of religious expression within Islam. It is important to recognize this diversity if one is to avoid making generalizations about all Muslims, but it is also important to understand that some of the less attractive voices within Islam are legitimately part of this spectrum. Statements such as, "Islam is a religion of peace", or "Islam is a religion of war", therefore, are too general to be meaningful. Some expressions of the Muslim faith, both contemporary and historical, are peaceful; others are not – neither group can claim to represent the whole spectrum that is Islam.

Islamism is a vibrant and dynamic aspect of the faith. The violent and extreme Muslims who have achieved such notoriety around the world are a legitimate part of the religion. Both the West and the moderate Muslim world need to face these streams if the *Umma* is to reform itself. It is important to recognize that this phenomenon of militarized religion is not merely a social or economic problem – it is a profoundly theological issue. The zealous young extremists are looking for theological certainty and assurance in a religion that can offer this only to those who die a martyr's death. When the conviction and passion that many radical Muslims demonstrate are comprehended within this ideological and theological context the violence can be effectively tackled.

Reforming zeal, when characterized as a return to the fundamental ideas or texts of a religion, need not necessarily be dangerous or violent. Only if the texts and traditions lend themselves to aggressive interpretation will violence ensue. Indeed, within Christian history the Reformation of the church in the 1500s came from a desire to return to the biblical texts. The militarized and corrupt practices of the medieval Catholic Church were eventually scrutinized and rejected precisely because Christian scriptures had been rediscovered. The crucial point then of any reformation is the content of a religious book, which if benign will inspire peace and forgiveness. In the same way zeal in itself need not be forceful or menacing. If passion and zeal are based upon positive ideals, these characteristics are crucial for the reform and improvement of a society.

Islamism has come into global consciousness through a series of high-profile terrorist events. By examining the Taliban movement, and other Islamist regimes, we have seen that the causes of Islamism are not only social and economic, but also profoundly theological. The case study of the Taliban, informed by much media attention, and also by our personal interaction with them, introduces some important characteristics of Islamism. The intensive politicization of religion, harsh insistence upon the *Shariah* law as the legal infrastructure at a national level and repression of women characterized the Taliban and other Islamist movements.

Islam is not a privatized religion, but has political action as an integral part of faithful practice. This foundation underlies the whole civilization and brings it into tension with others, which is illustrated by widespread antipathy to the power and influence of Western civilization, not without justification.

We have already argued that a Reformation-like change from within the *Umma* is one sought-after solution to aggression. However, just as the politicization of Islam needs to be critiqued by the *Umma*, so our Western cultural ideals need to be examined for what they are. Only then can we respond thoughtfully to the critiques provided by the extreme face of Islam – by the charges of decadence, of greed unchecked, of being a culture with an empty hole in its religious and thought life. These shortcomings are recognizable to many. However, it is important to reaffirm that to speak of "the West" is not to speak of "Christianity". Indeed where a "Western" response to Islamic extremism may be political or military, the response of the individual Christian must, after the example of Christ, and the teaching of the Christian Scriptures, be one of peace, love, forgiveness and the offer of the gospel.

At the heart of the Christian message is the good news of Jesus Christ and the value of humans made in the image of God – each is precious, whatever their ideology. God's love for every person ever conceived compelled him to reveal himself in the person of Jesus Christ. To this end he endured the evil of the world, the abuse of power, the corruption of government and judiciary, poverty, frailty and illness. God did not leave us with only a written word, but the "Word became flesh and lived among us" – and ultimately died among us.

The good news is that death could not hold him and Jesus burst from the tomb so that every human being could be reconciled to God. Humanity's hunger for purpose, assurance, salvation, rest and destiny are not vain imaginings, but find their fulfilment in Jesus. In the cross and resurrection there lies a solution to the human condition – namely forgiveness and the beginning of a relationship with God. The love and assurance found in Christ are certain because they are not based on human effort, but rather on sublime divine initiative. And so we end this book by commending you to this great mercy, this dynamic relationship, this offer of forgiveness from God through Jesus Christ.

Bibliography

Adly, Ibrahim, *Contours of Islamic Theology*, (Unpublished).

Ahmed, Akbar S., *Discovering Islam Making Sense of Muslim History and Society*, New York: Routlege, 1989.

Ahmed, Leila, *Women and Gender in Islam: Historical Roots of a Modern Debate*, Yale: Yale University Press, 1992.

Al-Bukhari, *The Translation of the Meaning of Sahih*, Al-Bukhari trans. Muhammad Muhshin Khan, vol. 6, al-Medina: Islamic University, 1983.

Al Qaradawi, Yusaf, *Islamic Awakening Between Rejection and Extremism*, London: International Islamic Publishing, 1995.

Arberry, A.J., *The Koran Interpreted*, Oxford: Oxford University Press, 1983.

Arberry, A.J., *Revelation and Reason in Islam*, London: George Allen & Unwin, 1957.

Aston, Margaret, Were the Lollards a Sect? in *The Medieval Church: Universities, Heresy and Religious Life* – Studies in Church History: Subsidia 11, Ecclesiatical History Society, Boydell Press, 1999.

Aston, Margaret, *Faith and Fire*, London: Hambledon Press, 1993.

Auda, Gehad, The Normalisation of the Islamic Movement in Egypt from the 1970s to the Early 1990s, in eds. Marty & Appleby *Accounting for Fundamentalisms: The Dynamic Character of Movements*, Chicago: University of Chicago Press, 1994.

Baran, A, Two Roads to Revolutionary Shi'ite Fundament-alism in Iraq, in eds. Marty & Appleby *Accounting for*

Fundamentalisms: The Dynamic Character of Movements, Chicago: University of Chicago Press, 1994.

Barr, James, "Fundamentalism" and Evangelical Scholarship, *Anvil*, 8/2: 141–52.

Barzun, Jacques, *From Dawn to Decadence*, London: Harper Collins, 2001.

Bostick, C.V., The Antichrist and the Lollards: Apocalypticism, in *Late Medieval and Reformation England*, Leiden: Brill, 1998.

Catto, Jeremy, Fellows and Helpers: The religious identity of the followers of Wycliff, in *The Medieval Church: Universities, Heresy and Religious Life*, Studies in Church History; Subsidia 11. Ecclesiatical History Society, Boydell Press, 1999.

Cox, Harvey, *Religion in the Secular City: Toward a Postmodern Theology*, New York: Simon and Schuster, 1984.

Cragg, K. and Speight, R.M., *The House of Islam*, California: Wadsworth Inc., 1988.

Cragg, K. and Speight, R.M., *Islam From Within*, California: Wadsworth Inc., 1980.

Dashti, Ali, *Twenty Three Years: A study of the Prophetic Career of Muhammad*, London: Allen & Unwin, 1985.

Eshghipour, Kourosh, The Islamic Revolution's Impact on the Legal and Social Status of Iranian Women, in *New England International & Comparative Law Annual*. http://www.nesl.edu/annual/vol3/iran.htm

Fuller and Lesser, *A Sense of Siege: the geopolitics of radical Islam and the West*, Colorado: Westview Press, 1995.

Gatje, Helmut, *The Qur'an and its Exegesis*, Oxford: One World, 1997.

Geisler, Norman, & Saleeb, Abdul, *Answering Islam: The Crescent in the Life of the Cross*, Michigan: Baker Books, 1995.

Goldziher, Ignaz, *Introduction to Islamic Theology and Law*, Princeton: Princeton University Press, 1981.

Goodwin, Jan, *Price of Honor: Muslim Women Lift the Veil of Silence on the Islamic World*, Plume, 1994.

Guillaume, A., *The Life of Muhammad: a translation from Ibn Hisham's* adaptation of Ishaq's Sirat Rasul Allah, Oxford: OUP, 1987.

Haykal, Muhammad Husayn, *The Life of Muhammad*, Indianapolis: N America Trust Publications, 1976.

Hunter, S, *Iran After Khomeini*, Prager, 1992.

Huntingdon, Samuel, *The Clash of Civilizations and the Remaking of World Order*, New York: Simon & Schuster, 1996.

Irwin, Robert, Islam and the Crusades, in *The Crusades*, ed. Riley-Smith.

Jedin, H. and Dolan, J., *History of the Church Volume IV*, London: Burns and Oates, 1980.

Jeffrey, Arthur, *Islam: Muhammad and His Religion*, New York: Liberal Arts Press, 1958.

Kabbani, Rana, *Letter to Christendom*, London: Virago, 1989.

Kane, O, Izala: The Rise of Muslim Reformism in Northern Nigeria, in eds. Marty & Appleby, *Accounting for Fundamentalisms: The Dynamic Character of Movements*, Chicago: University of Chicago Press, 1994.

Kepel, Gilles, *The Prophet and the Pharaoh. Muslim Extremism in Egypt*, Al Saqi Books, 1985.

Khurshid, Ahmad, Islam and the West: Confrontation or Cooperation? *The Muslim World* 85, Jan–April, 1995.

Leff, Gordon, *Heresy in the later Middle Ages Volume II*, Manchester: Manchester University Press, 1967.

Legrain, J.F., Palestinian Islamisms: Patriotism as a Condition of their Expansion, in eds. Marty & Appleby, *Accounting for Fundamentalisms: The Dynamic Character of Movements*, Chicago: University of Chicago Press, 1994.

Loserth, Johannes, *Wycliff and Hus* (Translated Evans, M.J., London: Hodder and Stoughton, 1884).

Luther, Martin, *Commentarius in Apocalypsin ante Centum Annos aeditus*, Wittenberg, 1528.

Mallouhi, C.A., *Waging Peace on Islam*, London: Monarch, 2001.

McFarlane, K.B., *John Wycliff and the Beginnings of English Nonconformity*, London: English Universities Press, 1972.

Mernissi, Fatima, *The Veil and the Male Elite: A Feminist Interpretation of Women's Rights in Islam*, Reading: Addison-Weasley, 1991.

Mernissi, Fatima, *Beyond the Veil: Male–Female Dynamics in a Modern Muslim Society*, Al Saqi Books, 1985.

Mitchell, Richard P., *The Society of the Muslim Brothers*, Oxford: Oxford University Press, 1993.

Monshipouri, Mahmood, The West's encounter with Islam, *Journal of Church and State*, Winter, 1998.

Nasr, Sayyid Hossein, *Ideals and Realities of Islam*, London: George Allen & Unwin; Boston: Beacon Press, 1966.

Nazir-Ali, Michael, *Frontiers in Muslim-Christian Encounter*, Oxford: Regnum Books, 1987.

Noll, Mark, *The Scandal of the Evangelical Mind*, Leicester: IVP, 1994.

Olesen, Asta, *Islam and Politics in Afghanistan*, London: Curzon Press, 1995.

Pearce, Joseph, *Solzhenitsyn: A Soul in Exile*, London: Harper Collins, 1999.

Pipes, Daniel, *Distinguishing between Islam and Islamism*, Center for Strategic and International Studies, June 30, 1998.

Pipes, Daniel, The Western Mind of Radical Islam, *First Things*, 58, December 1995.

Piscatori, J., Accounting for Islamic Fundamentalisms, in eds. Marty & Appleby *Accounting for Fundamentalisms: The Dynamic Character of Movements*, Chicago: University of Chicago Press, 1994.

Poole, R.L., *Wycliff and Movements for Reform*, London: Longmans, Green and Co., 1889.

Qutb, Sayyid, *Signposts: Beirut – Cairo*, The World Islamic Union of Students, 1980.

Rahman, *Islam: Challenges and Opportunities*.

Rashid, Ahmed, *Taliban Islam, Oil and the New Great Game in Central Asia*, London: Tauris Publishers, 2000.

Riley-Smith, Jonathan, *The Crusades: A Short History*, London: Athalone Press, 1987.

Rippin, Andrew, *Muslims Their Religious Beliefs and Practices Volume 1 The Formative Period*, London: Routlege, 1990.

Rippin, Andrew, *Muslims Their Religious Beliefs and Practices Volume 2 The Contemporary Period*, London: Routlege, 1993.

Roberts, H, From Radical Mission to Equivocal Ambition: The Expansion and Manipulation of Algerian Islamism, 1979–1992, in eds. Marty & Appleby *Accounting for Fundamentalisms: The*

Dynamic Character of Movements, Chicago: University of Chicago Press, 1994.

Roy, Olivier, *Afghanistan, From Holy War to Civil War*, Princeton: Princeton University Press, 1995.

Roy, Olivier, *The Failure of Political Islam*, London: Tauris Publishers, 1994.

Roy, Olivier, *Islam and Resistance in Afghanistan*, Cambridge: Cambridge University Press, 1986.

Sahebjam, Freidoune, *The Stoning of Soraya M.* Arcade, 1990.

Saroyan, M, Authority and Community in Soviet Islam, in eds. Marty & Appleby *Accounting for Fundamentalisms: The Dynamic Character of Movements*, Chicago: University of Chicago Press, 1994.

Schimmel, Annemarie, *And Muhammad is His Messenger*, Chapel Hill and London: The University of North Carolina Press, 1985.

Sergeant, L., *John Wyclif: Last of the Schoolmen and first of the English Reformers*, London: Putnam, 1893.

Sharma, Arvind, *Women in World Religions*, New York: State University of New York Press, 1987.

Shawcross, William, *The Shah's Last Ride*, Simon & Schuster, 1988.

Shepard, William, *Comments on Bruce Lawrence's "Defenders of God"*, Religion, 1992, Vol. 22, 279–285.

Shepherd, William, *"Fundamentalism": Christian and Islamic*, Religion; 1987, Vol. 17, 355–378.

Siddiqi, A.H., *Jihad* in Islam: A Comprehensive View, in *Criterion* Part I, III November–December, 1968.

Stacey, John, *John Wyclif and Reform*, London: Lutterworth Press, 1964.

Stowasser, B.F., *Women in the Qur'an, Traditions and Interpretation*, Oxford: Oxford University Press, 1994.

Vaughan, Robert, ed. *Tracts and Treatises of John de Wycliff*, The Wycliff Society, London: Blackburn and Pardon, 1845.

Walther, Wiebke, *Women in Islam*, Princeton: Markus Wiener Publishers, 1993.

Watt, Montgomery, *Muhammad Prophet and Statesman*, Oxford: Oxford University Press, 1961.

Watt, Montgomery, *Muhammad at Medina*, Oxford: The Clarendon Press, 1956.

Welch, A.T. and Cachia, P., *Islam: Past Influence and Present Challenge*, Edinburgh: Edinburgh University Press, 1979.

Wensinck, A.J., *Muhammad and the Jews of Medina*, Freiburg: Schwarz, 1975.

Wiktorowicz, Quintan, State Power and the Regulation of Islam in Jordan, *Journal of Church and State*, Autumn 1999.

Winn, H.E., ed. *Wyclif: Select English Writings*, Oxford: Oxford University Press, 1929.

Workman, H.B., *John Wyclif: a Study of the English Medieval Church*, Oxford: Clarendon Press, 1926.

Yousufzai, Rahimullah, Dostum unearths mass graves, *News*, 16 November 1997.

Yousufzai, Rahimullah. *News*, 2 February 1995.

Zolan, Alexander J., *The Effects of Islamization on the Legal and Social State of Women in Iran*, Int'l & Comp. L. Rev. 183, 1987.

Appendix

The Ninety-Nine Beautiful Names of Allah

Tradition relates that Muhammad once commented "there are ninety-nine names of God and whoever recites them will enter paradise." However, there are a number of different formulations in Islamic thought as to which these ninety-nine actually are. Below is one traditional formulation of the ninety-nine names of Allah.

Name/ Transliteration	Translation	Some verses from the Qur'an
ALLÂH	Allah	(1:1) (3:18) (5:109) (6:124) (7:180) (8:40) (16:91) (20:8) (57:5) (65:3) (74:56) (85:20)
AR-RAHMÂN	The Most Compassion-ate, The Beneficent, The Gracious	(1:3) (17:110) (19:58) (21:112) (27:30) (36:52) (50:33) (55:1) (59:22) (78:38)
AR-RAHÎM	The Merciful	(2:163) (3:31) (4:100) (5:3) (5:98) (11:41) (12:53) (12:64) (26:9) (30:5) (36:58)
AL-MALIK	The King	(20:114) (23:116) (59:23) (62:1) (114:2)
AL-QUDDÛS	The Most Holy	(59:23) (62:1)

AS-SALÂM	The All-Peaceful, The Bestower of Peace	(59:23)
AL-MU'MIN	The Granter of Security	(59:23)
AL-MUHAYMIN	The Protector	(59:23)
AL-'AZÎZ	The Mighty	(3:6) (4:158) (9:40) (9:71) (48:7) (59:23) (61:1)
AL-JABBÂR	The Compeller	(59:23)
AL-MUTAKABBIR	Supreme in Greatness, The Majestic	(59:23)
AL-KHÂLIQ	The Creator	(6:102) (13:16) (39:62) (40:62) (59:24)
AL-BÂRI'	The Maker	(59:24)
AL-MUSAWWIR	The Bestower of Form, The Shaper	(59:24)
AL-GAFFÂR	The Forgiver	(20:82) (38:66) (39:5) (40:42) (71:10)
AL-QAHHÂR	The Subduer	(13:16) (14:48) (38:65) (39:4) (40:16)
AL-WAHHÂB	The Bestower	(3:8) (38:9) (38:35)
AR-RAZZÂQ	The Provider	(51:58)
AL-FATTÂH	The Opener, The Judge	(34:26)
AL-'ALÎM	The All-Knowing	(2:158) (3:92) (4:35) (24:41) (33:40) (35:38) (57:6)
AL-QÂBID	The Withholder	(2:245)
AL-BÂSIT	The Expander	(2:245)
AL-KHÂFID	The Abaser	
AR-RÂFI'	The Exalter	
AL-MU'IZZ	The Bestower of Honour	(3:26)

AL-MUDHILL	The Humiliator	(3:26)
AS-SAMÎ'	The All-Hearing	(2:127) (2:137) (2:256) (8:17) (49:1)
AL-BASÎR	The All-Seeing	(4:58) (17:1) (42:11) (42:27) (57:4) (67:19)
AL-HAKAM	The Judge	(22:69)
AL-'ADL	The Just, The Equitable	
AL-LATÎF	The Gentle, The Knower of Subtleties	(6:103) (22:63) (31:16) (33:34) (67:14)
AL-KHABÎR	The All-Aware	(6:18) (17:30) (49:13) (59:18) (63:11)
AL-HALÎM	The Forbearing	(2:225) (2:235) (17:44) (22:59) (35:41)
AL-'AZÎM	The Incomparably Great	(2:255) (42:4) (56:96)
AL-GAFÛR	The Forgiving	(2:173) (8:69) (16:110) (41:32) (60:7)
ASH-SHAKÛR	The Appreciative	(35:30) (35:34) (42:23) (64:17)
AL-'ALIYY	The Most High	(2:255) (4:34) (31:30) (42:4) (42:51)
AL-KABÎR	The Most Great	(13:9) (22:62) (31:30) (34:23) (40:12)
AL-HAFÎZ	The Preserver	(11:57) (34:21) (42:6)
AL-MUGHÎTH	The Sustainer	
AL-HASÎB	The Reckoner	(4:6) (4:86) (33:39)
AL-JALÎL	The Majestic, The Revered, The Sublime	
AL-KARÎM	The Generous	(27:40) (82:6)
AR-RAQÎB	The Watchful	(4:1) (5:117)
AL-MUJÎB	The Responsive	(11:61)

AL-WÂSI'	The All-Encompassing, The All-Embracing	(2:115) (2:261) (2:268) (3:73) (5:54)
AL-HAKÎM	The Wise	(2:129) (2:260) (31:27) (46:2) (57:1) (66:2)
AL-WADÛD	The Loving One	(11:90) (85:14)
AL-MAJÎD	The Most Glorious	(11:73)
AL-BÂ'ITH	The Resurrector	(22:7) page 35
ASH-SHAHÎD	The Witness	(4:79) (4:166) (22:17) (41:53)(48:28)
AL-HAQQ	The Truth	(6:62)(22:6)(23:116)(31:30)
AL-WAKÎL	The Ultimate Trustee, The Disposer of Affairs	(3:173) (4:171) (28:28) (33:3) (73:9)
AL-QAWIYY	The Most Strong	(22:40) (22:74) (42:19) (57:25) (58:21)
AL-MATÎN	The Firm One, The Authoritative	(51:58)
AL-WALIYY	The Protector	(3:68) (4:45) (7:196) (42:28) (45:19)
AL-HAMÎD	The All-Praised, The Praiseworthy	(14:1) (14:8) (31:12) (31:26) (41:42)
AL-MUHSÎ	The Reckoner	
AL-MUBDI'	The Originator	(10:4) (10:34) (27:64) (29:19) (85:13)
AL-MU'ÎD	The Restorer to Life	(10:4) (10:34) (27:64) (29:19) (85:13)
AL-MUHYÎ	The Giver of Life	(3:156) (7:158) (15:23) (30:50) (57:2)

AL-MUMÎT	The Causer of Death	(3:156) (7:158) (15:23) (57:2)
AL-HAYY	The Ever-Living	(2:255) (3:2) (20:111) (25:58) (40:65)
AL-QAYYÛM	The Self-Existing by Whom all Subsist	(2:255) (3:2) (20:111)
AL-WÂJID	The Self-Sufficient, The All-Perceiving	
AL-MÂJID	The Glorified	
AL-WÂHID	The One	(2:163) (5:73) (9:31) (18:110) (37:4)
AS-SAMAD	The Eternally Besought	(112:2)
AL-QÂDIR	The Omnipotent, The Able	(6:65) (36:81) (46:33) (75:40) (86:8)
AL-MUQTADIR	The Powerful	(18:45) (54:42) (54:55)
AL-MUQADDIM	The Expediter	
AL- MU'AKHKHIR	The Delayer	(71:4)
AL-AWWAL	The First	(57:3)
AL-ÂKHIR	The Last	(57:3)
AZ-ZÂHIR	The Manifest	(57:3)
AL-BÂTIN	The Hidden	(57:3)
AL-WÂLÎ	The Governor, The Protector	
AL-MUTA'ÂLÎ	The Most Exalted	(13:9)
AL-BARR	The Benign, The Source of All-Goodness	(52:28)
AT-TAWWÂB	The Granter and Accepter of Repentence	(2:37) (2:128) (4:64) (49:12) (110:3)

AL- MUNTAQIM	The Lord of Retribution, The Avenger	(32:22) (43:41) (44:16)
AL-'AFUWW	The Pardoner	(4:99) (4:149) (22:60)
AR-RA'ÛF	The Most Kind, The Clement	(3:30) (9:117) (57:9) (59:10)
MÂLIK-UL-MULK	Owner of the Kingdom	(3:26)
DHUL JALÂL WAL IKRÂM	Possessor of Majesty and Honour	(55:27) (55:78)
AL-MUQSIT	The Just, The Equitable	(3:18)
AL-JÂME'	The Gatherer	(3:9)
AL-GHANIYY	The All-Sufficient	(2:263) (3:97) (39:7) (47:38) (57:24)
AL-MUGHNÎ	The Enricher	(9:28)
AL-MÂNI'	The Preventer of Harm	
AD-DÂRR	The Afflicter	
AN-NÂFI'	The Benefiter	
AN-NÛR	The Light	(24:35)
AL-HÂDÎ	The Guide	(25:31)
AL-BADÎ'	The Originator	(2:117) (6:101)
AL-BÂQÎ	The Everlasting	(55:27)
AL-WÂRITH	The Ultimate Inheritor	(15:23)
AR-RASHÎD	The Guide	
AS-SABÛR	The Patient One	

There are a number of different formulations of the Ninety-Nine Names.